Walking with BILBO

A devotional adventure through

The Hobbit

S A R A H   A R T H U R

Tyndale House Publishers, Inc.
Wheaton, Illinois

For my husband, Tom,
my treasured companion
for the journey

Visit Tyndale's thirsty Web site at areUthirsty.com

Visit www.saraharthur.com to learn more about Sarah Arthur.

thirsty(?) and the thirsty(?) logo are trademarks of Tyndale House Publishers, Inc.

Designed by Luke Daab

Arthur, Sarah.
    Walking with Bilbo : a devotional adventure through J. R. R. Tolkien's The Hobbit / Sarah Arthur.
        p. cm.
    Includes bibliographical references.
    ISBN 1-4143-0131-6 (sc)
    1. Tolkien, J. R. R. (John Ronald Reuel), 1892-1973. Hobbit.
2. Tolkien, J. R. R. (John Ronald Reuel), 1892-1973—Religion.   3. Fantasy fiction, English—History and criticism.   4. Middle Earth (Imaginary place)
5. Spiritual life in literature.   6. Religion in literature.   I. Title.
    PR6039.O32H63 2005
    823'.912—dc22   2004018964

Printed in the United States of America
10   09   08   07   06   05
6   5   4   3   2   1

WHAT'S INSIDE

A NOTE FROM THE AUTHOR

Over the past year since writing *Walking with Frodo,* I've had the opportunity to meet LOTR junkies of all stripes. Most of the time I've found myself among kindred spirits who enjoy the story in the same way I do: as great entertainment and excellent food for thought but without the level of importance of, say, world hunger. But occasionally I've found myself a stranger in a strange land, surrounded by Tolkien aficionados who know more about Middle-earth and the events of the Third Age than they do about the Middle East and the events of our time.

This is clear when I arrive at a speaking engagement to find several members of my audience deeply engrossed in a game of chess on a special edition *Lord of the Rings* board. Upon noticing my arrival, they greet me in Elvish. During the course of my talk, they correct me while I'm speaking: "Well, actually, Frodo was Bilbo's *first* cousin once removed on his mother's side and *second* cousin once removed on his father's side"; and during the Q & A time, they ask questions like "Some people insist that the books never say elves have pointy ears; could you expound on that?"

Yeah, I can expound on that. But that's not all I care about. I'm pretty sure that's not all Tolkien cared about either, though he loved to annotate his writings with endless footnotes and appendices, diving ever deeper into the complex history and mythology of his imaginary world. But back in the 1960s, when his American fans

were going loopy about hobbits and forming
communes in California where they lived in
holes and went around barefoot and got married
in Elvish, Tolkien got a bit irritated.

And no wonder Tolkien, a devout Roman
Catholic who took things like the marriage
ceremony seriously, referred to those fans as
his "deplorable cultus." In other words, their
cultlike attempt to replace reality with fantasy
was taking things down a road Tolkien never
intended.

At the same time, this misplaced devotion
highlights a crucial point that we dare not overlook: The story touches something deep down
inside us. It grabs hold of us on a spiritual level.
As author C. S. Lewis once said of another work
of fantasy, "It gets under our skin, hits us at
a level deeper than our thoughts or even our
passions, troubles oldest certainties till all questions are reopened, and in general shocks us more
fully awake than we are for most of our lives."[1]

Naturally we want to respond somehow, to
absorb the details of such a story like a sponge,

maybe even to use them as an escape from the real world of ordinary, mundane things. But unless someone challenges us to think about more than just the surface issues (e.g., whether or not the elves had pointy ears), we may miss the timeless truths and teachable moments that have the power to overhaul the way we live our lives in the real world.

In other words, it's not that the Tolkien aficionados take things too far; it's that they don't take things *far enough*. If we're going to take anything seriously in Tolkien's stories— if we're going to get really "religious" about it— we must consider the author's worldview.

Tolkien was a Christian, which he felt could be "deduced" from his stories.[2] Though he didn't set out to write an allegory and resented any attempt to make it so, he did become aware in the course of revision that the story's foundational themes were primarily Christian (rather than pagan)[3] and that those themes can be both significant and applicable[4] to our lives in the real world.

It's this applicability that was the focus of my first book, *Walking with Frodo*. Through a series of eighteen devotionals, I looked at the choices Tolkien's characters face in *The Lord of the Rings*, examined the spiritual implications of those choices, and then applied those truths to the decisions we make every day. In exploring the motives—both positive and negative—of Tolkien's characters, I find that our own motives are exposed. We find ourselves being challenged to examine each step we take on this journey and weigh its soundness.

Yet now it's time to take the process of examination even further. We need to go back to the beginning of the journey itself and investigate what got us started on this adventure of faith in the first place. In other words, while we must carefully consider our *choices*, we must also explore how and why we are *chosen*.

Enter Bilbo.

The hero of *The Hobbit* may seem an unlikely candidate for profound spiritual reflection. His tale, originally geared for children but enjoyed by all ages, is not the tortured, complex quest that we find in *The Lord of the Rings.* It's simply a fun-loving, lighthearted adventure that seems primarily concerned with when our hero will get his next meal (a serious issue for hobbits). Yet without the tummy-rumbling Bilbo, hand-picked by Gandalf as the "chosen and selected burglar," the events of *The Lord of the Rings* never would have taken place. Bilbo's very *chosen-ness* and his subsequent response have much to teach us about what it means to be called for a pur-pose larger than we could ever dream or imagine.

What starts us on the adventure? What does God see in us that we can't yet see in ourselves? How do we rise to the challenges we face along the road? What do we learn about ourselves and others when the unexpected happens, when our fellow companions fail us, when we reach the end of our strength and abilities, when we find ourselves in the dark?

Now *that* I can expound on!

—Sarah Arthur

READ THIS FIRST

*"It's a dangerous business, Frodo, going out of your door,"
he used to say. "You step into the Road, and if you
don't keep your feet, there is no knowing where you
might be swept off to."*

FRODO, QUOTING BILBO IN *The Fellowship of the Ring*,
BOOK ONE, CHAPTER THREE

If you prefer a safe, comfortable existence, by all
means don't read this book. Seriously. Shut it
right now and step away.

On the other hand, if you're ready for a riotous romp through the uncharted territory over the Edge of the Wild, into the landscape of your own soul: GET READY. It's a dangerous business opening the pages of a book—even more dangerous than stepping out your front door. Your life may never be the same again.

Bilbo should know. Many decades before the events of *The Lord of the Rings,* when he was still considered a fairly "young" hobbit (midfifties!), adventure came—literally—knocking at his door. Not just any adventure, mind you, but a treasure hunt in which one of two outcomes was inevitable: (1) death, or (2) riches beyond his wildest dreams. Considering the odds, a "sensible" fellow would have stayed at home in his snug hobbit-hole. But Bilbo, in spite of himself, took the plunge, though he wasn't keen on it at first. Upon learning that the dwarves were preparing to leave without him, he ran out of the front door of Bag-End at a full sprint, and so begins the story known as *The Hobbit.*

We have much to learn from Bilbo. Who said

life was about being sensible and snug, anyway?
Backpackers know you don't get the really cool
views staying down in the valley, all cozy in your
cabin. The unforgettable adventures with bears
and eagles and (dare we say) *dragons* don't happen
when you're cuddled up on the couch, snoozing
in front of the fire, or sitting at the kitchen table,
casually enjoying Second or Third Breakfast.
You have to be willing to take the risk, pack
your bags, hit the road, even miss a good meal
or two, in order to have the kinds of experiences
that will rock your world and change your life.

In short, you must be willing to set out on an
adventure, not necessarily a real expedition involving maps and transportation and luggage and
accommodations (though some of us are called
to that kind of experience as well), but an inward
journey of the soul. It's the kind that involves
confronting your own weaknesses as well as
strengths, going on when you're discouraged,
telling the truth when you don't want to, taking
responsibility for situations that require action,
overcoming the greedy desire to have the coolest

stuff, and sticking to the wisest path in the midst of conflict. These experiences test the very foundation of what you believe about who you are. Not only that, but they test what you believe about the One who got you started on this adventure in the first place: God.

Simply put, God specializes in sending people on adventures. We see this throughout the Bible: We have Abram (Abraham) and Sarai (Sarah), instructed to pack up house and move to a foreign country. Then there's Joseph, sold into slavery by his brothers and sent to Egypt; and Moses, chosen by God to free the Hebrew slaves and take them to the Promised Land. Or Jonah, the guy who was swallowed by a great fish when he attempted to flee in the direction opposite what God had in mind. And we can't forget Paul who went on a spiritual quest of inner transformation before being sent to the far corners of the known world as the first Christian missionary.

Most important, we have Jesus himself, who was on the road continually throughout the years of his ministry. Right from the start, he hand-selected a group of unlikely heroes for the expedition—disciples who left their safe, predictable existence in order to plunge over the Edge of the Wild. It's an invitation he extends to each of us today.

Faith is an ongoing adventure, not just a one-time choice: "The road goes ever on and on," as Bilbo regularly reminded Frodo. Once we hear the knock on the door and step onto the road, there's no turning back. Life will never be the same again.

Are you ready for the adventure?

Look! Here I stand at the door and knock.
If you hear me calling and open the door, I will come in,
and we will share a meal as friends.

REVELATION 3:20

bow to use this book

For those who first encountered Tolkien's imaginary world through *The Lord of the Rings,* reading
The Hobbit is the next logical step in attempting
to quench a thirst for more of Middle-earth.
And it's much less involved! Tolkien originally
wrote it as a children's story, so it's a quick, fun
read. If you've never read it before, find a copy
at your local bookstore or library, grab yourself a
hot mug of tea, and settle in for an unforgettable

adventure. And if you *have* read it before, it wouldn't hurt to peruse it again as you dive into *Walking with Bilbo.*

As you read, give yourself time to reflect on Bilbo's journey from a spiritual perspective. That's where *Walking with Bilbo* comes in. It can help guide you in the process of reflection as it follows the basic outline of Bilbo's adventure from beginning to end. From a biblical perspective, it also explores the experiences of the disciples who set out on the adventure of faith with Jesus about two thousand years ago. While Tolkien clearly didn't intend direct parallels between Bilbo and those first Christians, we can see many of the same principles at work in their experiences—and in our own as disciples today.

Walking with Bilbo is created to be a devotional guide, which means there are short readings based on events in *The Hobbit,* followed by "Going Further" questions for reflection, and related Bible passages. You will want to (a) be familiar with *The Hobbit,* as already mentioned;

(b) grab a pen or pencil to jot down your thoughts for the "Going Further" questions; and (c) have a Bible handy (the New Living Translation is used for this book). If at times you can't keep track of characters or places in Tolkien's stories, there is a "Quick Reference Guide" in the back of this book.

It's also essential to be familiar with the books or movies of *The Lord of the Rings* trilogy, particularly *The Fellowship of the Ring.* There we see Bilbo many years after his adventures in *The Hobbit;* there too we see the inevitable results of his "accidental" finding of the Ring.

And finally, for a wonderful explanation from Gandalf's point of view regarding his selection of Bilbo for the expedition to the Lonely Mountain, Tolkien's tale "The Quest of Erebor" is also highly recommended.[5]

Thoughts to Get You Started
What lessons or opportunities would Bilbo have missed out on if he had decided to stay home instead of accepting the journey's challenge?

What are some of the ways Bilbo's journey changed him?

How do you know when God is calling you to the adventure of faith? What does his "knock" sound like on the door of your soul? How do you hear his voice?

What does following Jesus look like today? How tempting is it to maintain a "safe, comfortable existence" rather than follow Jesus? What might someone miss out on if he or she doesn't choose to follow Jesus?

What are you going to do about it?

LOOKING
FOR A FEW
GOOD MEN
(OR HOBBITS)

"I am looking for someone to share in an adventure that I am arranging, and it's very difficult to find anyone."

GANDALF, CHAPTER ONE OF *The Hobbit*

Remember those awful middle school gym classes when the teacher selected two captains and told them to take turns picking their team-mates, one at a time? Either the captains' voices were drowned by the clamoring throng ("Pick me! Pick me!"), or their words echoed in an uncomfortable silence ("I want her but not him; and you, over there—No, not *you*."). Any twinge of sympathy for those left standing till the end was quickly overpowered by the extreme relief at not being one of them. How unfair it seems that certain people should be chosen (for some of the silliest reasons, too) while others aren't!

Then of course, there's the wretched classroom lecture scenario, usually involving a subject in which you feel hopelessly stupid. While the instructor paces around the podium, you sit quietly in your seat, trying not to move or sneeze or in any way draw attention to yourself. Because you know the firing squad of questions is coming. The instructor will wheel around suddenly and aim a zinger at some poor, unsuspecting student who may or may not have the fortitude to answer. And you hope it won't be you. *(Please don't pick me. PLEASE.)* How unfair it seems that every student will be chosen at some point, including you!

Hmm. Interesting to compare the two scenarios, isn't it? In the first, you're desperate to get the attention of the person in charge rather than suffer the embarrassment of not being selected. In the second, you're desperate to stay under the radar altogether. But in both situations, you'll end up getting chosen eventually. The issue isn't whether or not you'll be chosen; the issue is *when*.

For Mr. Bilbo Baggins—who is about to be selected by one of the most famous captains in all literature—the time is *now*. Gandalf is in something of a hurry, and the little hobbit doesn't appear to be doing anything important at the moment. If he'd had his wits about him, Bilbo would've disappeared inside his hobbit-hole the minute he saw Gandalf coming. (*Please don't pick me. PLEASE.*) But besides being completely unaware of Gandalf's intentions, Bilbo is also—deep down—an adventurous fellow, though he doesn't realize it yet.

In fact, there are a great many things he doesn't realize, as Gandalf well knows. The wizard tells the dwarves, "There is a lot more in him than you guess, and a deal more than he has any idea of himself."[6] Bilbo is being chosen precisely because Gandalf sees something in him that needs only the "chance to come out," and an adventure will do the job nicely. Despite Bilbo's protests—as well as those of the dwarves—he becomes the "chosen and selected burglar" for the expedition to the Lonely Mountain.

Chosen and selected. The words have a nice ring, don't they? They make us sit up a bit taller, lift our chins a little. Even if, like Bilbo, we're not sure what the words *mean* exactly, we rather like the idea of being handpicked for a purpose. It's not simply because we're susceptible to flattery, like the dragon, Smaug. Deep down we long to know that we have value and worth in someone's eyes, that someone thinks we have a role to play in the stories of our time.

And Someone does. The Creator of the

universe is also the Creator of every human life, including yours, and all that he does has a purpose. God made you for a reason and has a plan for your life. He's calling you to fulfill a purpose within a story that is larger than you could ever dream or imagine: an adventure beyond all adventures!

God had been in the business of hand-selecting people for specific jobs since the beginning of time. He cranked the recruitment process into high gear when Jesus came on the scene. Picture Peter with his brother Andrew, mending fishing nets on the shores of an inland sea. Peter doesn't have much in the way of education, nor is he what you might consider . . . um, shall we say, *prudent*. But Jesus says, "Come, be my disciples" (Matthew 4:19), and off he goes, Andrew at his side. Drop everything? Now? Okay. The rest of the twelve disciples have similar responses, and before long, voilà: you have an organized expedition.

Frankly, if you're really not interested in

adventures, it's wise to hide when you see Jesus coming. He has Gandalf-like tendencies that are really quite alarming. "Follow me," he says. "Take nothing for your journey. Go the extra mile. Why do you worry about what you will eat or what you will wear? Seek first God's kingdom." These are not safe words. At the very least, they could "make you late for dinner." In fact, they might mean you don't get any dinner at all.

But Jesus also says to his disciples, "You didn't choose me. I chose you" (John 15:16). This adventure of faith may appear to have a rather dubious origin and an even more dubious outcome, but that doesn't trump the fact that in this moment, in this hour, you are being called to walk with Jesus.

The question is, will you go?

Long ago, even before he made the world, God loved us and chose us in Christ.

EPHESIANS 1:4

GOING FURTHER

⊕ What tasks have you been "chosen and selected" for? Why were you chosen?

⊕ How does it feel to be asked?

⊕ How does God view you? How easy or difficult is it to see yourself the way God sees you?

⊕ Why has God chosen and selected you for the adventure of faith?

⊕ What are you going to do about it?

THE WORD ON BEING CHOSEN

Take some time to read one or more of the following Bible passages:

Deuteronomy 7:6-8; Isaiah 6:8 and 41:9-10; Mark 2:13-17; Luke 6:12-16; James 2:5; 1 Peter 2:9

JOB DESCRIPTION, PLEASE

> *"Burglar wants a good job, plenty of Excitement and reasonable Reward. . . ."*
>
> GLOIN, INTERPRETING THE MARK GANDALF INSCRIBED ON BILBO'S FRONT DOOR, CHAPTER ONE OF *The Hobbit*

Just under one hundred years ago, a British explorer by the name of Sir Ernest Shackleton embarked on an expedition to the Antarctic aboard a wooden sailing vessel named the *Endurance.* To recruit crew members for this dangerous mission, it's said he placed an advertisement in a London newspaper that ran something like this:

MEN WANTED FOR HAZARDOUS JOURNEY. SMALL WAGES, BITTER COLD, LONG MONTHS OF COMPLETE DARKNESS, CONSTANT DANGER, SAFE RETURN DOUBTFUL. HONOUR AND RECOGNITION IN CASE OF SUCCESS. SIR ERNEST SHACKLETON.[7]

At least he was honest. At most, he gained a remarkable crew who survived some of the most brutal conditions imaginable, long after the expedition went horribly wrong and the *Endurance* broke apart in the ice. The tale of their survival will not soon be forgotten: They endured twenty-two months trekking across moving pack ice, sailing in open lifeboats, and being stranded on bleak islands—and not one of the twenty-eight crew members was lost.

But what if Shackleton had written a different

job description? What if, out of fear he wouldn't get any takers, he'd painted a rosier picture, glossing over reality?

MEN WANTED FOR OCEAN CRUISE. SPLENDID SAILING VESSEL, GOOD BENEFITS, GREAT VIEWS, EXOTIC WILDLIFE. HONOUR AND RECOGNITION UPON RETURN HOME.

It's not hard to imagine what sort of response he would have received: dapper dandies with their streamlined luggage and state-of-the-art camera equipment, inquiring into whether the main entrée would be shrimp or filet mignon. It's also not hard to imagine the outcome of *that* expedition.

Clearly, it's good to know what you're getting into before you accept a job. What will be expected of you, exactly? What are the benefits? Is this a part-time or full-time position? Short-term or long-term? Are there any hazards or personal safety concerns? The sensible person inquires into these details up front.

If Bilbo is anything in the opening pages of *The Hobbit*, it's sensible. When the dwarves first discuss the implications of their expedition and then turn to Bilbo as their "professional" burglar, he inquires into the job description: "I should like to know about risks, out-of-pocket expenses, time required and remuneration, and so forth."[8] Tolkien adds that this is Bilbo's way of asking, "What am I going to get out of it?" And "Am I going to come back alive?"

Considering what Bilbo is being asked to do (travel many miles through dangerous lands to steal back treasure from a deadly dragon), it's not as though he fits the job description. In fact, he's never stolen anything in his life, much less gone into the business of professional burglary as a full-time vocation. And though Gandalf has his own reasons for choosing him, it's clear that Bilbo (a) is currently unqualified for the position and (b) doesn't want it to begin with. Yet even as

he protests his title of Professional Burglar, he
finds himself wanting to "live up to Gandalf's
recommendation." In short, when hard-pressed,
he's willing to give it a shot.

Aha! We've stumbled upon one of Tolkien's
important themes in both *The Hobbit* and *The Lord
of the Rings:* If you want an important job done,
you don't give it to the professionals. You seek
out the little folk, the overlooked, the small and
insignificant. You choose those who may not, on
the surface of things, have much to recommend
them but whose characters have hidden potential
that the rest of the world does not see. Tolkien
wrote that he "saw the value of Hobbits . . . in
providing subjects for 'ennoblement' and heroes
more praiseworthy than the professionals."[9]
A hobbit might balk at the job description, but
he'll stick to it till the bitter end.

We often feel like hobbits in the wild world
of faith. Open the pages of the Bible and you
find story after story of God choosing the small,
the unsuspecting, the unqualified. Think about

people like Joseph, Moses, David, Esther, and
Paul—all selected precisely because they seemed
the least likely. Joseph? He was a slave. Moses?
He had murdered a man. David? He was the
least of his brothers, far too young to be king
of Israel. Esther? She probably would be killed
if she entered the king's presence without his
invitation. And Paul? He persecuted Christians
as a full-time job. Yet in time we see the wisdom
of God's choice in each one of these characters.

The twelve disciples were a motley bunch too.
If Jesus had wanted, he could have selected any
number of priests and scholars and teachers—
the real professionals. And if *they* hadn't been
willing, there was a host of everyday, ordinary
people who followed him at first, from town
to town, miracle to miracle. To some, listening
to him may have been cheap entertainment,
and many of the poor and disenfranchised had
nothing better to do.

But when some of them inquired into the job
description for Lifelong Follower, they turned

away in fear. The whole thing sounded so . . . uncomfortable. *Now that you mention it, where does Jesus sleep if he's constantly on the road, anyway? What does he eat if he has no home or family? You mean there's no guarantee about dinner? Thanks, but no thanks!*

No one can say Jesus glossed over the job description. When people had the guts to inquire into following him, he replied with disconcerting things like "If you cling to your life, you will lose it; but if you give it up for me, you will find it" (Matthew 10:39). Hmm. Doesn't sound like a job with a lot of benefits, does it? Or what about this: "Go and sell all you have and give the money to the poor, and you will have treasure in heaven. Then come, follow me" (Matthew 19:21). Ouch. Talk about out-of-pocket expenses!

Perhaps that's why Jesus didn't choose the professionals to be his twelve disciples; he chose those who were willing to do the job. Most of them were uneducated. Several were political rebels. At least one was deeply disliked by most people because of his profession as a tax collector. All were sinners. But the one thing they had in common was a willingness to give it a shot. Jesus saw something in them that they couldn't yet see in themselves, and that was enough. They got the job.

So if you're feeling a little unqualified lately, if you're slightly queasy about the details of God's classified ad, take heart. Like Bilbo, you've been called for a reason. The job of following Jesus isn't for the faint of heart; but God never would call you if he didn't plan to strengthen your heart along the way.

Remember, dear brothers and sisters, that few of you were wise in the world's eyes, or powerful, or wealthy when God called you. Instead, God deliberately chose things the world considers foolish in order to shame those who think they are wise. And he chose those who are powerless to shame those who are powerful. God chose things despised by the world, things counted as nothing

at all, and used them to bring to nothing what the world
considers important, so that no one can ever boast
in the presence of God.

1 CORINTHIANS 1:26-29

GOING FURTHER

⊕ How tempting is it to turn down God's offer when you hear the job description for following Jesus?

⊕ What specific tasks is God asking you to do right now that you're hesitant about? If you're hesitating, why?

⊕ When you follow through on what God wants you to do, what do you learn about yourself? about God?

⊕ What if God calls you to stay put—to stick it out in a difficult relationship, an unfulfilling job, or a frustrating family situation? What are you going to do about it?

THE WORD ON ACCEPTING THE JOB

Take some time to read one or more of the following
Bible passages:

Exodus 3:10-14; 1 Samuel 16:6-12; Esther 4:13-17;
Jeremiah 29:11; Luke 14:25-33

CHAPTER THREE

SHEER MADNESS

He may have lost the neighbours' respect, but he gained—
well, you will see whether he gained anything in the end.

FROM CHAPTER ONE OF *The Hobbit*

"Mad Baggins": that's what they call him.

By the time the events of *The Lord of the Rings* begin, Bilbo's reputation has long since been ruined by his sudden disappearance on that spring morning over half a century before— and his equally sudden reappearance. Only

Frodo seems to understand his elder cousin's adventurous streak and doesn't seem to mind that Bilbo's reputation has rubbed off on him. Everyone, except for maybe Sam Gamgee, who accompanies Frodo on the journey to destroy the Ring, assumes the Bagginses are crazy.

Bilbo's shenanigans on his eleventy-first birthday, as chronicled in the opening scenes of *The Fellowship of the Ring*, simply solidify his neighbors' suspicions. Only crazy people go off on adventures from which they don't return for years. Only those who are "cracked" go off and do something like disappear in plain view (or, should we say, *from* plain view), never to be seen by their neighbors again. In other words, if you want to stay respectable and maintain your reputation, hanging out with a Baggins is not a good idea.

It's an age-old story. The world doesn't know what to do with fools. Most of the time, we ostracize those who step out of line, do something extraordinary, challenge the social

norms. People like that make us feel uncomfortable, and if there's anything we hate, it's being
uncomfortable. We're especially alarmed when
we ourselves are seized by the mad (yes, *mad*)
urge to do something unexpected, to break away
from the pack and take off into some unknown
adventure. We'd prefer to stifle those feelings
and go on with our safe—if boring—existence.
We have reputations to maintain, right?

Funny how God doesn't care much about
reputations! He calls folks who have horrible
pasts to follow him, and he calls others to ruin
their reputations altogether—in the eyes of
their neighbors, anyway—for the sake of his
Kingdom. In God's eyes, there's no higher calling than to be a fool for Christ, though of
course the ultimate paradox is that the more
foolish we appear as people of faith, the wiser
we probably are.

But we don't always feel that way. Like
Bilbo—who can't, for the life of him, figure
out *why* he takes off running after the dwarves

(without hat or money or pocket-handkerchief, mind you)—we often question the wisdom of this belief business. Certainly the Christian faith is both reasonable and plausible. Many intelligent, thinking people throughout the centuries have accepted the claims of Christ, including Tolkien himself and his colleague C. S. Lewis.[10] But it certainly isn't considered *normal* or *accepted*, especially if you allow it to change the entire direction of your life and let it interfere with your everyday activities.

The disciples heard the call of Christ and left everything to follow him. It's possible some of their family members were a little irritated. Their neighbors probably gossiped behind their backs. Perhaps at times they felt twinges of doubt themselves, especially when Jesus said and did things that seemed outside of the bounds even *they* had set for him. For example, when Jesus was pressed by the crowds to do another miracle, as he had with the loaves and fish, he said, "I am the bread of life. . . . All who eat my flesh and drink my blood remain in me, and I in them" (see John 6:47-59). *Wait,* the disciples likely thought, *did he just say "drink my blood"? I think he did. Hello?! Does he imagine we're barbarians or something?*

In fact, the Bible says that "at this point many of his disciples turned away and deserted him" (verse 66). Even though the twelve "chosen and selected" disciples remained, things had taken a decidedly uncomfortable turn. The journey most likely would get worse before it got any better. Several of them proba- bly considered calling it quits altogether. But then Jesus looked at them and asked, "Are you going to leave, too?" (verse 67).

How would *you* respond?

Disciples today also experience moments in which this whole faith thing seems like madness. There are days when the words of Jesus or the prayers we pray or sermons we hear in church or the rituals of Communion and baptism seem utterly absurd. Yes, let's be honest. Life would be a whole lot easier if we didn't have to take all

those things so *seriously*, wouldn't it? And most
people choose not to.

But at some point it becomes obvious that,
ultimately, the adventure of faith is the most
sensible thing to do, and in fact the only thing
worth doing. As Sam says toward the end of *The
Two Towers*, no one remembers the tales in which
the characters give up and turn back. Great and
heroic deeds remain undone if no one leaps into
the dark to do them. That's true when it comes
to faith, too. You can't play a meaningful role in
the great story by playing it safe. Once you hit
the road, there's no going back to life as it was
before. When Jesus asks the disciples if *they* will
leave him too, Peter says, "Lord, to whom would
we go?" (verse 68). It's either walk with Jesus,
crazy as it seems sometimes, or go home.

In the end, you're not really crazy, of course.
You're in fact one of the wise ones in this world,
willing to trust your welfare and your future
to the One who gave you life and called you to
follow Jesus. Like "Mad Baggins," you many not

earn your neighbors' respect, but you'll gain the richest reward imaginable.

This "foolish" plan of God is far wiser than the wisest
of human plans, and God's weakness is far stronger
than the greatest of human strength.

1 CORINTHIANS 1:25

GOING FURTHER

⊕ How important is your reputation—your desire to conform to what everyone else thinks is "cool"? Be honest.

⊕ Why might faith in Jesus Christ seem foolish to the rest of the world? What does it mean to be wise in God's eyes?

⊕ When does faith seem foolish to you?

⊕ How do those moments of doubt affect your willingness to follow Jesus?

⊕ What are you going to do about it?

THE WORD ON BEING
WISE IN GOD'S EYES

Take some time to read one or more of the following
Bible passages:

Proverbs 3:1-4 and 3:21-26; Acts 26:24-29;
1 Corinthians 1:18-25, 2:14, 3:18-20, and 4:10-13;
Ephesians 5:15-17

CHAPTER
FOUR

TRAVELING LIGHT

"I'm awfully sorry," said Bilbo, "but I have come without my hat, and I have left my pocket-handkerchief behind, and I haven't got any money."

FROM CHAPTER TWO OF *The Hobbit*

If backpacking were a competitive sport, the winner would not be the hiker who trekked the farthest distance in the least amount of time. It would be the guy with the lightest pack.

Yep, the real gearheads will tell you it's not about how many peaks you bag or how many miles you haul or how trashed your boots are, but about how many pounds you've managed to skim off your pack by keeping only the ounces that count. Your sleeping bag weighs over three pounds? Ditch it. Buy the latest high-tech, high-loft, ounce-crunching model and wow your companions in camp at night. Only idiots bring things like canned soup. Dehydrate, dehydrate, dehydrate, baby. Do you know how much water *weighs?* Rumor has it the real minimalists even saw off the ends of their toothbrushes.*

Needless to say, when it comes to packing light for long-distance travel, Bilbo Baggins wins the prize. This doesn't mean he's particularly happy about it. After plunging out the front door of Bag-End with nothing but the clothes on his back, he arrives breathless for the scheduled departure more than a little annoyed with himself—and with everyone else, for that matter. The dwarves are kind enough to lend him the essentials, but it's Gandalf who sees to the details.

*This author's husband doesn't even *bring* a toothbrush. Ew!

Bilbo doesn't really *need* his pocket-handkerchief
and other accessories; they're minor niceties to
make the trip more pleasant when the road gets
difficult. But Gandalf knows what makes a
hobbit a happy (or at least a happi*er*) camper.

In fact, Gandalf knows a lot more about these
creatures called hobbits than most of the movers
and shakers of his time. He has a good grasp
on Bilbo's heritage as both a Baggins and a
Took: The Baggins side of Bilbo prefers to stay
at home where a warm bed and good food are
the norm, while his Took side (related through
his mother's family to the infamous Pippin
of later tales) longs for a little adventure. The
question is, when the road gets tough, will Bilbo
resort to being a Baggins, refusing to go another
step without a good pocket-handkerchief, or
will he rise to being a Took, brave and resource-
ful in the midst of hardship?

Gandalf knows that he must coax Bilbo's
Tookish nature to the fore if the expedition is
to succeed. But he also knows he can't ignore the

Baggins side altogether, at least not at first. The hobbit's griping and complaining might turn into outright mutiny if pushed too far. So Gandalf paces the journey and makes sure Bilbo's basic needs are being met before the real hardships begin. And slowly but surely we begin to see Bilbo's Tookish side rise to the challenge.

If we're honest, there's more than a little Baggins in each of us. We all like our creature comforts. Even retailers who sell backpacking gear are aware of this principle. Their shelves are crammed with tempting gadgets for making life a little cozier on the trail. Take the featherlight espresso maker, for example. Or the nifty nozzle that turns your water bladder into a backcountry shower. Does the serious hiker actually need these things? Not really. And eventually the hiker realizes these things will in fact impede his travel, add to his feelings of exhaustion, and keep him focused on the next stop rather than on what he's experiencing along the trail.

When it comes down to it, we're fools for

anything that takes the edge off life's inevitable
trials and pains. That explains why we have a
hard time distinguishing what we *need* from what
we *want*. Like Bilbo, we have a tendency to lump
hats and money and pocket-handkerchiefs in the
general category of Crucial Necessities, without
making a distinction between those items upon
which *life itself* depends and those items upon
which only our *happiness* depends. It takes seasons
of real struggle and hardship before we're able
to put it all in perspective.

It's not hard to imagine that's exactly what
God has in mind. Like Gandalf, God knows
the battle going on inside our hobbitlike selves,
the wrestling match between the Baggins and the
Took. The Baggins side of us takes our creature
comforts for granted. We assume these comforts
are part of the terms and conditions outlined
in the job description Jesus offers when he says,
"Follow me." But God never said anything about
discipleship being *comfortable*. He's more interested
in coaxing the Took side of us to the fore, the

side that's willing to endure a little hardship for the sake of the final destination. When we learn to live without, we discover what we're really made of.

When Jesus was preparing to send the disciples out into the countryside as missionaries and itinerant preachers, he instructed them to "take nothing with them except a walking stick—no food, no traveler's bag, no money. He told them to wear sandals but not to take even an extra coat" (Mark 6:8-9). Did he expect them to starve or freeze, or what? No, he expected them to rely completely on God to provide for all of their needs. And because they had no luggage to haul around or stuff to keep track of, they were free to be spontaneous, open to accepting kindness from strangers, and able to be more effective in what they set out to accomplish.

God asks us to travel light for a reason. Our spiritual journey can be impeded by excess. The more stuff we haul along that is meant to bring us comfort, the more difficult the adventure of faith becomes. We begin to focus on when we can stop and take a break from the various tasks God asks us to do rather than on learning to enjoy the tasks themselves. Like Bilbo, if we're not careful, our love for creature comforts could hold us back from the adventure of faith altogether.

Your heavenly Father already knows all your needs,
and he will give you all you need from day to day
if you live for him and make the Kingdom
of God your primary concern.

MATTHEW 6:32-33

GOING FURTHER

⊕ When have you doubted God's concern for your well-being? What happened?

⊕ How hard is it to distinguish between the things you need and the things you want? When you're

packing for a trip? When you're shopping?
When you're praying?

⊕ What creature comforts would be hard for you
to live without? Why?

⊕ In what ways do these creature comforts keep
you from pursuing God's plan for your life?
What would it take for you to give those up?

⊕ What are you going to do about it?

THE WORD ON BEING
WELL-PROVIDED FOR

Take some time to read one or more of the following
Bible passages:

Exodus 16:1-5; 1 Kings 17:2-16; Psalm 147:7-11;
Matthew 6:25-33; Luke 12:22-31; Acts 2:44-45;
Philippians 4:6

NOW YOU
SEE HIM, NOW
YOU DON'T

"Just when a wizard would have been most useful, too."
DORI AND NORI, CHAPTER TWO OF *The Hobbit*

Where *is* Gandalf, anyway?

Not far into chapter 2 the dwarves' intrepid leader is nowhere to be found, reappearing only just in time to save the entire company from being squashed and eaten by trolls. Later he's conspicuously absent when the goblins capture the company in the mountain cave, and again, he comes to their rescue when things get bad. Still later he bids them good-bye on the edge of Mirkwood, at perhaps the most dangerous stage of their journey. In fact, it's one of the wizard's trademark characteristics throughout *The Hobbit* to be absent just when Bilbo and the others think they need him most. Needless to say, the company is not at all pleased.

But in time we begin to sense that Gandalf's absences have a purpose. He doesn't always intend to be gone, of course; sometimes he has pressing business to attend to. At other times, as Tolkien hints later in chapter 9, Gandalf's absences might in fact be planned, in order to allow for Bilbo and the dwarves to rise to the challenges they face. Hobbits and dwarves are mighty courageous when put to the test but mighty reticent to be tested. They'd prefer to let the professionals handle the really sticky situations while they sit comfortably on the sidelines. But Gandalf isn't about to let them.

There's a spiritual lesson here, as you probably guessed. But before we get too involved, we must remember that Tolkien's stories are not meant to be allegories. There is not a one-to-one correlation between characters, places, or events in *The Hobbit* and the characters, places, or events in the biblical narrative; nor can you substitute Gandalf, the coordinator of the expedition to the Lonely Mountain, with Jesus, the One who calls us to follow him on the journey of faith. Unlike Jesus, Gandalf is limited and fallible, capable of poor judgment and miscalculation. But at times Gandalf's behavior *reminds* us of God's activity in our lives and gives us the opportunity to reflect on our spiritual journey.

This "now you see him, now you don't" experience sounds familiar to those who have chosen to walk with Jesus. Our Fearless Leader, on whose presence we depend for our very survival, has the alarming tendency to "disappear" just when things get difficult—or so it seems to us. We can go for long stretches during

which Christ's presence is very real and palpable:
We hear him speak through Scripture; we chatter
to him in prayer; we even sense his companionship in our everyday routine. But then, without
warning, we feel horribly alone. We call out, but
we hear no one. The words of Scripture seem
cold; our prayers are met with a vast, eerie silence
from heaven.

For centuries theologians have wrestled with
this aspect of human experience. Intellectually,
we know that God is present everywhere; no
one is beyond the reach of his presence. And
as Christians we know that Jesus dwells within
us through the power of the Holy Spirit. One
of the last recorded things Jesus says to his disciples are these words of reassurance: "Be sure
of this: I am with you always, even to the end
of the age" (Matthew 28:20). So how do we
explain those times when we feel utterly alone?
What do we do when, in our darkest hour,
we see no glimmers of light anywhere and our
prayers seem to go unanswered?

Even the disciples—who walked and talked with Jesus and experienced his companionship on a daily basis—had moments when they felt totally abandoned. Take the incident of the storm on the Sea of Galilee, for example (see Mark 6:45-51 or Matthew 14:22-33). After a long, busy day of ministry, Jesus instructs his disciples to leave without him and take a boat to the other side of the lake. Meanwhile, he goes into the hills to pray for the night. Eventually a storm kicks up and it becomes clear that the disciples will never make it to the other side without help. We can imagine what they're thinking and feeling in this moment: *He told us to leave without him, and here we are. There's no possible way he can save us now. We might as well die.*

They don't die, of course, but you'll have to read the story to find out what happens! The point is they are alone. Jesus deliberately leaves them on their own. Then at the last possible moment, when they've done everything they know to do, he finally appears.

There will be times when you, too, feel alone in this journey of faith. Maybe it's when you lose a loved one or when you feel the sting of rejection from friends you thought you could trust. It may happen if you struggle with depression and feel lost in a dark fog that never seems to lift. Perhaps it's simply the inexplicable feeling that God has left for a long trip and won't be back for some time. Whatever the case, *hang in there.* You are not alone. God has promised to "neither fail you nor forsake you" (Deuteronomy 31:6).

In Tolkien's narrative, Bilbo and the dwarves learn in time to keep going on, whether Gandalf appears to be available or not, and to keep their hopes up even when they feel abandoned. They are not *really* alone. Help always comes. As the Elvenking says to Gandalf at the end, "May you ever appear where you are most needed and least expected!"[11]

It's not that God abandons us ever, much less for long stretches of time; it's that our own limited human nature occasionally keeps us from feeling God is near. Sin, emotional numbness, demands of this world . . . these are at times barriers between the human soul and the experience of God's presence. But there will come a day—at the end of all days—when we will finally see him face-to-face. It will no longer be "now we see him, now we don't." It will be *now we see him.* Forever.

> *Be sure of this: I am with you always,*
> *even to the end of the age.*
>
> MATTHEW 28:20

GOING FURTHER

⊕ When do you feel most alone?

⊕ How does it feel to know that God never abandons you?

⊕ What keeps you from experiencing God's presence in tough times?

⊕ What do those experiences teach you about yourself? about God?

⊕ How important is prayer during those times?

⊕ What are you going to do about it?

THE WORD ON FEELING FORSAKEN

Take some time to read one or more of the following Bible passages:

Deuteronomy 31:6; Psalm 27:7-10 and 138:8; 2 Corinthians 4:9; Hebrews 13:5-6

CHAPTER SIX

PLANS GO ASTRAY

Even the good plans of wise wizards like Gandalf and of good friends like Elrond go astray sometimes when you are off on dangerous adventures over the Edge of the Wild; and Gandalf was a wise enough wizard to know it.

FROM CHAPTER FOUR OF *The Hobbit*

So what are your plans for tomorrow? Seriously, what's on your calendar for the day? Perhaps it's a regular program of school or work or household chores with a level of predictability to your schedule: get up, take a shower, get dressed, eat breakfast, prop yourself up with a little caffeine, head to whatever it is you do every day, move through the regular routine, etc. Or maybe it's the weekend, in which case the routine shifts and there are perhaps more open blocks of time to be spontaneous. Whatever the case, it's important to ask yourself this question: Can I say with reasonable certainty that things will go as planned?

When you stop and think about it, how predictable *is* life? All of us can remember a day when an unexpected event threw off our entire routine—if not our entire existence. Perhaps it was a life-altering phone call about the illness or death of a loved one. Maybe it was only a temporary frustration, such as the hot-water heater breaking down in your dorm or the fire alarm going off at 2 a.m. Even the most carefully crafted vacation contains elements of surprise: a detour on the highway, a delayed plane, a lost reservation, a missing piece of luggage.

We cannot confidently predict what each day of our lives will hold, though our calendars are full of activities carefully recorded on almost every line of available space. This inability to predict what's coming is especially true when we've left the normal routine and set out on the journey of faith. We may have a rough idea of what's in store, but this is an *adventure* after all, and if you could predict the events that take place at every stage in the journey, the story wouldn't really be worth telling, would it?

This brings us once again to the unexpected and unpredictable adventure of Mr. Bilbo Baggins.

Tolkien doesn't tell us much about the company's visit in chapter 3 to the Last Homely House, Master Elrond's abode in Rivendell. The author's explanation is that peaceful days hold little interest to the readers of an adventure story. True enough! So Tolkien skips to the discussion about Thorin's map and then soon after that to the next stage of their journey.

After Rivendell, it's time for the company to head into the mountains and the Wild. Yes, this is the same mountain chain that Frodo and the Fellowship encounter with Gandalf so many years later, though Bilbo's journey takes place far to the north of the Mines of Moria. But the scenario is almost exactly the same both times: The travelers head up the mountain trail and encounter a fierce storm that forces them to either take shelter (as in *The Hobbit*) or turn back (as in *The Fellowship of the Ring*). And both times they somehow end up *inside* a mountain, trapped within the realm of goblins (orcs) and unsure of how to escape alive.

But before any of this happens in *The Hobbit,* as the company gets closer and closer to the mountains, Gandalf suspects that "something unexpected might happen." Notice Tolkien's wonderful little joke: The *unexpected* is something that you don't expect. So if you expected it, it wouldn't be unexpected anymore! Yet we can relate to Gandalf's feeling of unease. *Something* is going to happen that you haven't planned for, but you're not sure what that something is.

Once again, we hear echoes of the gospel
narrative in this snippet of hobbit adventures
in Middle-earth—not because Tolkien intended
it, but because all adventure stories have this in
common: they're unpredictable. Life itself is a
plot that we can't guess or anticipate.

Jesus, the Master Storyteller, knew he had
to prepare his followers for the unexpected—
even for those things that, to their minds,
would seem disastrous but were part of God's
overall plan. Not only did he instruct his
followers to travel light and trust in God to
take care of them, Jesus warned about getting
too confident about what each day would
bring. Even the things they were looking
forward to, such as the return of the Messiah
to conquer their enemies and reclaim the throne
of the world, could not be mapped out on a
calendar. "Know this," he said: "A homeowner
who knew exactly when a burglar was coming
would not permit the house to be broken into.
You must be ready all the time, for the Son

of Man will come when least expected" (Luke 12:39-40).

But there also were impending events that the disciples wanted to avoid altogether, if possible, not the least of which was the very real possibility that Jesus could be arrested and even killed. Their sense of unease grew stronger as Jesus drew closer and closer to Jerusalem in those last weeks. Yet Jesus knew that whatever happened, God was in charge; they were in God's hands.

Lesson learned? A handful of clichés sum it up well: Life is not predictable. Expect the unexpected. As Gandalf understood, even the best-laid plans can fall apart. We do not know what tomorrow will bring, nor can we say with certainty what God is up to in our lives. But whatever the case, we are in God's hands, even when our plans appear to go astray.

We can make our plans, but the LORD determines our steps.

PROVERBS 16:9

GOING FURTHER

⊕ When it comes to your daily or weekly schedule, how confident are you that things will happen as planned?

⊕ How do you deal with the unexpected? How comfortable are you with life's unpredictability?

⊕ In what ways is God at work even when your best-laid plans fall apart?

⊕ How can you more thoroughly commit your plans to God and put yourself in his hands?

⊕ What are you going to do about it?

THE WORD ON MAKING PLANS

Take some time to read one or more of the following Bible passages:

Psalm 37:4-5 and 90:16-17; Proverbs 14:12, 16:3, and 27:1; Ecclesiastes 9:12; Matthew 6:34; Luke 12:16-21; James 4:13-17

CHAPTER
SEVEN

GOING ON

"Go back?" he thought. "No good at all! Go sideways?
Impossible! Go forward? Only thing to do!
On we go!"

Bilbo, Chapter Five of *The Hobbit*

The call always comes when you least expect it:
while you're blitzing to your next class down the
hall or loading laundry into the washing machine
or laughing with your friends during lunch.
Your cell phone buzzes, your beeper goes off,
or you come home to find the light blinking on
the answering machine. The message stops you

cold: Someone you dearly love is clinging to life in the ER. You must get there as quickly as possible. Without pausing to think, you switch your brain into autopilot and hit the road.

It occurs to you as the car speeds along that life will never be the same again, as much as you hope everything will be all right in the long run. Everyone in your family or circle of friends will be altered forever by this experience. There's no going back.

It also occurs to you that all the things you've been fussing and worrying about up to this moment seem utterly ridiculous. When it comes to the things that are *really* important in life, you've been sidetracked into all kinds of tangential issues that have no significance. You couldn't care about those issues right now, even if you tried. Stated briefly, there's no going sideways.

No going back. No going sideways. The only thing to do is to go forward into whatever this day brings. Plant one foot in front of the other, do what needs to be done, find the courage to face whatever you encounter along the way. There's only one other option—tempting, to be sure—and that's to stay where you are and refuse to move. As darkness descends upon your family, your community, your life, it's altogether possible that you simply could sit there and do nothing in response. But as all the great stories teach us, even *that* is not really an option—at least not for long.

Once again, we arrive at one of Tolkien's most important themes in his tales of Middle-earth, planted as a small seed taking root in Bilbo's story that grows into a major lesson in *The Lord of the Rings*.

Going on.

Perhaps the best example in all of Tolkien's stories is when Sam finds the body of his beloved Master Frodo, whom he believes is dead from an attack by the giant spider, Shelob. After the initial shock and grief, Sam begins pondering what must be done. He wonders, "But what can I do? Not leave Mr. Frodo dead, unburied on the

top of the mountains, and go home? Or go on?
Go on?"[12] Eventually he realizes that *is* his only
choice. He must resist despair, put one foot in
front of the other, and go on into the darkness.

It's interesting to note that while Tolkien was
writing these chapters of *The Lord of the Rings*, his
son Christopher was stationed with the Royal
Air Force in South Africa during World War
II. Tolkien sent parts of the manuscript to
Christopher, hoping it would provide some
relief from the monotony and futility of his
situation. Again and again in his letters, Tolkien
decried the darkness and hopelessness of war,
perhaps because of his own experience as a
young soldier in World War I. In many ways,
these chapters could be seen as his encouragement to Christopher to keep going, even though
all seemed dark around him. "Well, there you are:
a hobbit amongst the Urukhai," Tolkien wrote
to him: "Keep up your hobbitry in heart. . . ."[13]

Hobbits are stouthearted creatures, not easily
beaten down. In *The Hobbit*, we find Bilbo far less

inclined to give up and give in than his supposedly tough companions, the dwarves. When lost
and forgotten in the dark tunnels under the
Misty Mountains, in the midst of goblin territory, Bilbo determines that there's nothing else
for him to do but go on into the dark. Then
later, when in another tunnel in yet another
mountain, heading down toward the fire and
smoke of Smaug, he resists the urge to turn back.
Tolkien tells us that, for Bilbo, "Going on from
there was the bravest thing he ever did."[14]

Going on from there. How many times do we
struggle with mounting despair when the circumstances we find ourselves in seem too dark to
overcome? when a family member is ill, when our
friends turn their backs on us, or when we seem
to fail at everything we try? How tempting it is
to curl up, pull our hoods over our faces, and
remain where we are in the dark! And sometimes
God knows we need simply to sit and grieve—
and that's perfectly natural. But eventually he
calls us to get up, assess the situation, and move

forward. We may not be sure the direction we're headed is the right one, but we've used whatever common sense we can muster, trusting God to give us wisdom. The rest is in his hands.

Jesus knew this temptation to give up and give in. He felt it keenly in the garden of Gethsemane on the night of his arrest, when his enemies were coming to capture him and his life was in danger. He told his disciples, "My soul is crushed with grief to the point of death" (Mark 14:34). Then he went off by himself and prayed for God to "take this cup of suffering away" (14:36). But even as he said it, he knew there was no going back, no going sideways. If God wanted him to move forward into the darkness, he was willing: "Yet I want your will, not mine" (14:36). The rest was in God's hands.

The disciples, too, exemplified this dogged determinedness, as the book of Acts shows us. Often we picture them as spiritual superheroes, able to leap tall problems in a single bound. But they faced moments of discouragement and indecision, just as we do. The New Testament letters are full of Paul's words of encouragement: "You have suffered so much for the Good News. Surely it was not in vain, was it? Are you now going to just throw it all away?" (Galatians 3:4). We can safely say he wouldn't have written such words if the disciples hadn't needed to hear them!

These words of encouragement speak to us as well. The lesson is this: When the road gets dark and all hope seems lost, there's nothing to do but keep going. We, like Bilbo, must keep up our "hobbitry in heart." Even more important, as people of faith, we recognize that we are not alone. Whatever happens from this point on, we put our trust in God. And we go on.

We are pressed on every side by troubles, but we are not crushed and broken. We are perplexed, but we don't give up and quit. We are hunted down, but God never abandons us. We get knocked down, but we get up again and keep going.

2 CORINTHIANS 4:8-9

GOING FURTHER

- ⊕ What difficult circumstances are you facing right now?

- ⊕ When are you tempted to give up in the face of those circumstances? Why?

- ⊕ Where is God when all seems dark around you?

- ⊕ What encourages you to keep going?

- ⊕ What are you going to do about it?

THE WORD ABOUT GOING ON

Take some time to read one or more of the following Bible passages:

Psalm 69:1-3; Isaiah 35:3-4 and 40:27-31; Romans 5:3-5; 2 Corinthians 12:9-10; Galatians 6:9; 2 Thessalonians 3:13; 1 Peter 1:6-7

SEEKING AND
FINDING

*Suddenly his hand met what felt like a tiny ring of cold
metal lying on the floor of the tunnel. It was a turning
point in his career, but he did not know it.*

FROM CHAPTER FIVE OF *The Hobbit*

Have you ever found something you weren't
even looking for? Let's say you're walking across
a grassy lawn and glance down to see a four-leaf
clover. You crouch to get a better look, and sure
enough it's the real deal. Incredible! You could
spend days looking *on purpose* and never find one.

You pluck it, marveling at your tremendous good luck—whatever that means. Granted, you're probably not going to win the lottery after this. And yet there's something about the experience that makes you feel specially . . . *chosen* somehow.

Then of course, there are the times when you deliberately search for something that fails to appear. Perhaps it's an item you've lost—which you inevitably need *right now*—such as your hat or homework or car keys. (Whatever it is, chances are you're still looking for it.) Or maybe you search for a certain turn that shows up on the map but doesn't seem to exist anymore, as far as the known world is concerned. "It says *left*, right? But there is no left. This can't be right!" It makes you wonder how many exits have been missed since the beginning of highway transportation, how many millions of lonely items are moldering away in the lost-and-found bins of the world.

Seeking and finding, finding and losing: We've stumbled on yet another of Tolkien's major themes. His bumbling heroes are forever losing their way, losing each other, losing weight, all while trying to *find* their way to the Lonely Mountain and the treasure. But while they remain focused on seeking what they think is the ultimate prize, something of far greater worth slips in under their very noses. In what seems like an accident, Bilbo finds what he isn't even looking for, and not only is it "a turning point in his career," but it's the axis on which the entire history and future of Middle-earth revolves.

It's clear that not even Tolkien himself understood the significance of what Bilbo finds there in the dark of the tunnel—at least not at first. In fact, one of the most intriguing things about the text of *The Hobbit* and how Bilbo ends up with the Ring is that there are two versions of the story! The first, from the original 1937 edition, depicts the Ring as something of little significance, a handy accessory that renders Bilbo invisible when he and the dwarves get trapped in sticky situations. It's so insignificant, in fact, that Gollum agrees to *give* it to Bilbo as a

present if Bilbo wins the Riddle Game—though
he doesn't tell Bilbo what the present is just yet.
Gollum soon discovers he has lost the Ring
and thus can't keep up his end of the bargain,
so he agrees to show Bilbo the way out instead.
And that story remained in subsequent editions
of *The Hobbit* until the events of *The Fellowship
of the Ring* made it clear that no one, least of all
Gollum, would have the fortitude to give the
Ring away so casually![15]

So Tolkien wrote a new version of *The Hobbit*
in 1951, in which Gollum betrays Bilbo and tries
to hunt him down in the tunnels before he makes
his escape. In an upcoming chapter we'll discuss
how Tolkien accounted for this enormous difference between the two tales.[16] But meanwhile we
have some interesting things to discuss about
the nature of seeking and finding.

First, no tale of adventure would be all that
interesting if it didn't center upon some kind
of quest. A quest is a journey one takes in order
to find or gain something, such as the answer to

a *question*, an item of great worth, a timeless love, or a sense of belonging. The quest is the ultimate plot device for most of the world's great stories, including the story of all stories, the tale of our faith. That's because . . .

Second, every human soul—including yours—is on a quest for whatever satisfies; we are eternally restless to know how and why we're here on this planet and what the future holds for us. Stories of adventure speak to that longing in all of us. But in real life, many people don't even know what they're looking for. Some don't even know that they're looking!

Third, only in Jesus can we find what we seek. Saint Augustine prayed, "You have formed us for Yourself, and our hearts are restless till they find rest in You." Even though we were created to be with God from the beginning—to have our needs met within the loving circle of his care for us—we rebel against God and wander off to do our own thing. The problem is, nothing else can meet our needs the way God can. We try all kinds of things—relationships, the latest trends, popularity, success—in an effort to fill the emptiness inside us, but nothing works. We are restless until we return to God through Jesus Christ.

In Luke 15, Jesus tells his disciples three stories in a row about lost things of great worth that are eventually returned to their owners. The first is about a lost sheep: The shepherd leaves the rest of his flock in order to find the one that's missing. The second is about a lost coin: A woman sweeps her entire house to find it. The final story is one of the most famous of all time: A son rebels against his father, takes his share of the inheritance, and runs away to live on the wild side. In time he realizes he's been really stupid and returns to beg his father's forgiveness. Each story ends with a celebration—what was lost has been found.

The point is that God treasures each person so much that he's like the shepherd, like the woman with the missing coin, like the heartbroken father. He will stop at nothing to find those who are lost, and he throws a party upon their return. Not only that, but he calls each of us to follow his lead. We're to look diligently for those who have wandered away from God. It's one of our primary roles in this adventure of faith.

Jesus sent his disciples on a great treasure hunt to find the lost—a task he calls us to today. Like Bilbo, we often may feel like *we're* the ones who are missing in action, wandering in the dark. But in the meantime, we just might stumble across things of great value in the form of family or friends who need to find God and be found by him. The question is, will we recognize such treasure when we find it?

You will search again for the LORD your God. And if you search for him with all your heart and soul, you will find him.

DEUTERONOMY 4:29

GOING FURTHER

⊕ Think about someone or something important
to you. How would you feel if you lost that person
or thing, never to be part of your life again?

⊕ When have you felt lost or separated from God?
How did you respond to those circumstances?

⊕ What does it mean to be spiritually lost?

⊕ Who among your friends or family is spiritually
lost but doesn't know it? Who among them is
looking for God?

⊕ What are you going to do about it?

THE WORD ON SEEKING
AND FINDING

Take some time to read one or more of the following
Bible passages:

*Proverbs 2:1-8; Isaiah 65:1; Jeremiah 29:12-13;
Matthew 7:7-8 and 13:44-46; Luke 15:3-10; Acts
17:22-27*

CHAPTER NINE

FOR PITY'S SAKE

*A sudden understanding, a pity mixed with horror,
welled up in Bilbo's heart.*

FROM CHAPTER FIVE OF *The Hobbit*

If Bilbo's finding of the Ring is the "turning point in his career," then his decision to have pity on Gollum is the turning point upon which the fate and future of Middle-earth hang.

Think about it: What if he *does* go ahead and stab Gollum there in the dark? Gollum is out to kill him, we must remember. What if, out of self-defense, Bilbo takes advantage of the fact that Gollum is unarmed and unable to see him? Bilbo could easily justify his actions, saying his life is in danger. And besides, the world would be rid of a nasty, vile creature whose death would go completely unnoticed.

Yet think of the long string of events that would have followed this tiny decision through all three books and films of *The Lord of the Rings.* In the long-term view, we could say that, had Bilbo killed Gollum, the Dark Lord Sauron never would have discovered that the Ring still existed. Through Gollum, Sauron learned there was such a thing as hobbits, and one of them was Baggins, and Baggins had a Ring of Power. With this knowledge the Dark Riders were sent from Mordor to hunt for the land called the Shire, and at least one of them made it to the very threshold of Bag-End. If Gollum had died, Frodo wouldn't have suffered the wound that haunted him the rest of his life, nor been attacked by the giant spider, nor lost a finger. Nor would a great many other terrible things have happened.

But you could also say that, had Bilbo killed Gollum, a great many *good* things might never have happened either. Gandalf wouldn't have realized the urgency of sending Frodo on his journey when he did. He might have been content to let Frodo keep the Ring hidden and safe, and its power could have grown on Frodo; or Frodo might have surrendered it to the wise leaders of his time, who would have eventually yielded to its temptation. You could say that without Gollum, Frodo and Sam would have been lost forever in fog or drowned in the marshes or died at the hands of their enemies when attempting to enter the evil land of Mordor. They never would have crossed safely over the border at all, and the mission would have been doomed.

And of course, in the end, the Ring itself wouldn't have been destroyed. Middle-earth would have been lost forever.

So Bilbo's decision to have pity on Gollum, there in the tunnel under the Misty Mountains, is an event of far greater significance than anyone save Gandalf suspects. As the wizard says to Frodo years later, "My heart tells me that [Gollum] has some part to play yet, for good or ill, before the end; and when that comes, the pity of Bilbo may rule the fate of many—yours not least."[17] Frodo isn't convinced at first that Bilbo made the right choice all those long years ago, but he's willing to follow Bilbo's example and heed Gandalf's gentle reproof. During the course of his own journey, Frodo feels pity for Gollum and offers the creature mercy he doesn't deserve. It's an attitude Sam struggles to understand. Gollum is out to kill them when he gets the chance, just as he was out to destroy Bilbo so many years before. But by some strange mystery, even Sam feels pity for Gollum at the end and refuses to kill him when he has the chance.

How could this be? What is it about a hobbit

that says, "Even if you mean to kill me, I will let you live. You are forgiven"? How could a nasty character like Gollum—who betrayed the hobbits over and over again—be given a second, third, fourth chance?

It goes back to Bilbo's feeling of pity: the "sudden understanding" that allows him to see things from Gollum's point of view. Like Bilbo, Frodo and Sam are able to put themselves in Gollum's place and offer him the mercy they themselves would wish to be given.

A tough lesson, to be sure. We're not always too keen on practicing mercy ourselves. This is especially true when the Gollums in our lives go about their little betrayals: spreading bits of gossip at school, setting us up for failure on the job, dropping hints that we may not be as well liked as we suppose. We toss and turn in bed at night, rehearsing the crushing comment or the cruel look we will use the next time this person hurts us. Rarely do we ponder things from their perspective, even if we know or suspect they might have a tougher life than most. We fail to ask ourselves the crucial question: How would I want to be treated if I were in their shoes?

Jesus makes it clear to his disciples that those who wish to follow him must take the road of mercy. And like us, the disciples aren't too keen on this at first. As Jesus is speaking to a large crowd, he says, "But I say, don't resist an evil person! If you are slapped on the right cheek, turn the other, too" (Matthew 5:39). We can imagine the twelve disciples glancing uncomfortably at each other and then looking at the ground. *Okay, the guy's nice, but that's taking things a little too far.*

Pity and mercy. Pity is the feeling we have when we put ourselves in someone else's shoes. Mercy is the second chance we offer this person, even though it is not deserved. God responds in just this way to us—and where would we be if he didn't? Jesus says, "God blesses those who are merciful, for they will be shown mercy" (Matthew 5:7). In other words, our experience of God's grace grows in direct proportion to the grace we offer others. We may not look them in the eye and say it directly, but our actions are clear: *Even though you're doing your best to hurt me, I forgive you.*

It's a tough road, and one we'd rather avoid. But we can keep in mind Bilbo's choice. Who knows how the future of the world might be changed by that one small decision?

> *Stop judging others, and you will not be judged.*
> *For others will treat you as you treat them.*
> *Whatever measure you use in judging others,*
> *it will be used to measure how you are judged.*

MATTHEW 7:1-2

GOING FURTHER

⊕ What's the difference between pity and mercy? How are the two related?

⊕ In what ways have others extended mercy to you?

⊕ How easy or difficult is it for you to have pity
   toward others—to put yourself in their shoes?

⊕ Who in your life needs your mercy? Why?

⊕ What are you going to do about it?

THE WORD ON PITY AND MERCY

Take some time to read one or more of the following
Bible passages:

*Psalm 51:1-12 and 103:8-18; Isaiah 55:6-7; Jonah 3:10–
4:11; Matthew 18:21-35; Luke 18:9-14; Ephesians
2:4-7; James 2:12-13 and 4:11-12*

PORTENTS OF GREAT SIGNIFICANCE

This departure from truth on the part of a most honest hobbit was a portent of great significance.

FROM TOLKIEN'S FOREWORD TO THE REVISED EDITION
OF *The Hobbit*

Bilbo, as the prime example of his species, loves to have a good time. Granted, he finds it a bit tricky to have fun when there's not enough food in his tummy, but that doesn't stop him from pulling a practical joke when he gets the chance.

Shortly after he escapes from Gollum in the tunnels and comes upon his companions at the beginning of chapter 6, Bilbo pulls a fast one that makes the dwarves believe he's just as sly and light-footed as the burglar he's been hired to be. The whole thing is such a blast that he decides to keep the Ring a secret for a bit longer. Nothing like the prospect of a practical joke to keep your spirits up!

Ah, yes, a practical joke. For the Bilbo types among us—perhaps yourself included—it's hard to resist the opportunity. We all know the slumber party stories, when someone plastic-wrapped the toilet bowl or put shaving cream in toothpaste tubes or sent underwear up the flagpole. Need we mention Silly String? Time would fail us to tell of water balloons launched at just the right moment, answering machine messages sounding suspiciously like the president of the United States, or various incidents involving duct tape.

April Fools' Day in particular is prime time

for the more sophisticated kinds of jokes, most involving a slight . . . ahem . . . *departure from the truth.* The notice on official letterhead saying you've won a full ride to the college of your choice, for example; or, on the flip side, the announcement that you're fired. The tiny . . . um, *lie* . . . is only temporary, of course! That's the fun part. But that's where the joke stops. Once discovered, it certainly wouldn't be funny anymore if the joker were to keep acting like the whole thing was true. It would be annoying at first, and then . . . downright troubling.

Right from the start—even though he enjoys the joke—Gandalf suspects that "something's up" with Bilbo's story. Bilbo is an extraordinary hobbit, as Gandalf knows, but not *that* extraordinary—at least not yet. It would take a tremendous amount of courage for Bilbo to escape Gollum *and* the goblin guards with nothing but his little dagger to help him (a weapon he barely knows how to use, no less). There's more to the story than Bilbo is telling, and later we learn this puzzles Gandalf a great deal—worries him, in fact. He's even more worried when Bilbo finally admits to having found a Ring that makes its wearer invisible. Why didn't the honest hobbit mention it in the first place? And why does his story of the ending to the Riddle Game sound so . . . fishy?

As mentioned before, there's a huge discrepancy between the Riddle Game's outcome as it appeared in the 1937 edition of *The Hobbit* and the episode as it finally evolved when Tolkien began writing *The Lord of the Rings.* That Gollum would offer to give away the Ring as a present simply would not wash. So how was Tolkien to fix the problem? Would he write a long letter of explanation to his readers in the foreword of the next edition, saying something along the lines of, "I totally messed this up, so please ignore the section about the Riddle Game"? Not likely.

No, Tolkien had a more creative idea. Since *The Hobbit* was written supposedly by Bilbo himself, as a memoir of his travels, Tolkien would say that *Bilbo* had made the mistake. In fact, he would say Bilbo lied in his journal. The otherwise honest hobbit had carried on the practical joke well past the point of humor, all due to the disturbing, distorting influence of the Ring, and it was this "departure from the truth" that first alerted Gandalf to the Ring's unhealthy influence.

Tolkien called it a "portent of great significance." The word *portent* means a clue or a sign, usually something with an ominous tone. Those who aren't scoping for portents might easily overlook them. But Gandalf wasn't one to ignore such things. Something was not right, and Bilbo's not-so-little white lie was the clue.

Jesus, too, had the uncanny ability to uncover tiny discrepancies in human character. Behavior his followers viewed as relatively unim*port*ant was a thing of great significance to him—an ominous sign of inner spiritual decay that needed to be uncovered and dealt with. After telling a parable about honesty in regard to wise use of financial resources, he said, "Unless you are faithful in small matters, you won't be faithful in large ones. If you cheat even a little, you won't be honest with greater responsibilities" (Luke 16:10). It's a principle that applies to all areas of truth telling in our lives.

As followers of Jesus, we can't ignore it when a friend's story doesn't add up. At the very least, we need to explore: "If she's glossing over the truth regarding this issue, what else isn't she telling the truth about?" When we probe, we might discover other disturbing behaviors: She could be refusing to talk about crucial problems, avoiding friends who care, or hiding important issues from family. Whatever the case, she must be confronted before this departure from truth leads to a departure from faith altogether.

We learn in *The Lord of the Rings* that it was years before Gandalf finally confronted Bilbo with point-blank questions about the Riddle Game. And Bilbo was mighty reluctant to tell the truth at first. In fact, it wasn't until he gave up the Ring to Frodo—an act demonstrating, to Gandalf's relief, that the Ring's power hadn't corrupted Bilbo beyond recovery—that Bilbo was able to go public with the whole story. At the Council of Elrond in *The Fellowship of the Ring,* Bilbo said, "I will now tell the true story, and if some here have heard me tell it otherwise"—he looked sidelong at Gloin—"I ask them to forget it and forgive me."[18] In the end, Bilbo returned to the truth and became his dear old self again.

Suffice it to say, we'll have plenty of opportunities to laugh and have fun on this adventure of faith, but a lapse in character when we slip from the honesty God requires of us is not one of them. The sooner we deal with it the better, and the sooner we can return to the healthy, fun-loving people God created us to be.

Just as damaging as a mad man shooting a lethal weapon
is someone who lies to a friend and then says,
"I was only joking."

PROVERBS 26:18-19

GOING FURTHER

⊕ What happens when a joke is taken too far?

⊕ When have you noticed troubling signs, or "portents
of great significance," in a friend's or family
member's behavior? What do those signs tell you?
How can you help that person return to the truth?

⊕ When are you tempted to depart from the truth?
What does that tell you about yourself?

⊕ What are you going to do about it?

THE WORD ON DEPARTING
FROM THE TRUTH

Take some time to read one or more of the following
Bible passages:

*Genesis 3:1-13; Psalm 32:1-5; Proverbs 12:17-20;
Acts 5:1-11; Ephesians 4:14-15; 1 Peter 3:10*

BETWEEN A ROCK
AND A HARD
PLACE

"Escaping goblins to be caught by wolves!"

BILBO, CHAPTER SIX OF *The Hobbit*

So your friend has this little . . . habit. Well, it's
more like a problem. Okay, to be quite honest,
it's a very serious problem. It's called shoplifting.

He started when he was in middle school,
wanting to impress his friends and looking for a
touch of excitement after school when there was

nothing much to do. There was a sort of adrenaline rush to it. The more daring the theft, the bigger the rush. He and a couple of others began a competition to outdo each other, to push the line until someone got caught—though of course each of them thought he was far too clever for that to happen.

You've always been on the fringes, of course, not wanting to appear too condemning and earn your friend's disgust, but not wanting to participate either. He's gotten annoyed the few times you've attempted a lighthearted rebuke, so you try to ignore what he's doing, hoping he'll wise up, grow up, grow out of it. If possible, you avoid situations in which the two of you are in a store together.

Except today. He stops by the store for some food while giving you a ride home from class, and there's not really any way out of it. So you slouch into the store behind him, hoping he'll make for the dairy section like he's supposed to and then head to the checkout. But it's not to be.

As soon as you see what he's up to, you walk away, head down the next aisle, pretending to browse near the checkout lanes, waiting for him to show up with that weird, nervous grin on his face.

Then it occurs to you. You've just witnessed a *crime.* Is it okay for you to simply stand there without confronting him? Will your conscience let you do that? Will God? Sure, the guy's your friend. But a crime is a crime. And yet you hesitate. If you confront him—or if that fails, report him—you'll most likely lose a friend for life, and possibly a good many other friends too. But if you don't confront him, your conscience will never let it go. You'll be enabling his sinful behavior, ignoring an injustice against the owner of the store, and disappointing God. You're caught between a rock and a hard place, as the old saying goes. And neither option feels good.

At least in this scenario, there's a right choice, though it doesn't feel like it in the short term. But sometimes in the adventure of faith there will be circumstances outside of your control that demand action, requiring you to choose between two paths that both seem wrong, or at least painful, and you must do your best to reach a decision. As Madeleine L'Engle says, "Often we are put in positions where all of our choices are wrong; there is no *right* thing to do."[19] Somehow you must choose between the "lesser of two evils," between the rock and the hard place, and live with whatever happens next.

By chapter 6 of *The Hobbit*, we find Bilbo and Gandalf and the dwarves in just such a quandary. They're trapped in circumstances outside of their control and will be lucky to escape with their lives. And at the moment it looks like there's no chance of that. The evil wargs have "treed" them, even as the goblins track their trail after their escape from the tunnels. The company has gone from one bad situation to another—"out of the frying pan into the fire"—and things will get worse before (if!) they get better.

Gandalf has tried various tactics to forestall

the dwarves' inevitable demise (not to mention his own), but now there's nothing to do but pitch one last effort that likely will cost him his life. Much to our relief, he's rescued at the last moment.

The adventure of faith is not without its rocks and hard places—places where all choices seem wrong, or at least painful. Jesus himself faced enemies who did their best to set him up on purpose, to trap him with questions that seemed to have no "right" response so they'd have a reason to get him arrested.

One of the most famous examples is in the eighth chapter of John, when the religious teachers bring before him a woman who has been caught in adultery. "The law of Moses says to stone her," they tell him. "What do you say?" (verse 5). They're counting on his compassion to overrule his desire to follow God's commandments so they can accuse him of breaking the law. But Jesus instead poses a conundrum for *them* that will take some wiggling out of: "All right, stone her. But let those who have never sinned throw the first stones!" (verse 7). Ouch. Now *they're* caught between a rock and a hard place. The woman's accusers aren't stupid. They know that if they start stoning her, they're claiming to be sinless, which is a form of blaspheming God—only God is perfect and holy. But if they leave her alone, Jesus wins. And of course, either way, they still won't have a good enough reason to arrest the guy. It's just not fair!

They might have lost this one, but their tactics don't end there, of course, and soon we find Jesus praying in the garden of Gethsemane on the night of his arrest, asking God for strength to face the rock and the hard place, the frying pan and the fire. He knows his disciples will face such difficulties too, if they follow in his footsteps. By way of encouragement, he says to them, "Here on earth you will have many trials and sorrows. But take heart, because I have overcome the world" (John 16:33).

We don't often face circumstances that

endanger our lives no matter which way we turn, as is the case for Bilbo, Gandalf, and the dwarves in chapter 6 of *The Hobbit*. But we do face situations such as losing a friend, disappointing a parent, or failing to succeed—no matter what we do or say. It's just one of those unavoidable realities on the journey of faith. But we have this promise from the One in whose footsteps we follow: God can bring good out of both the rock *and* the hard place. God honors our willingness to do the best we possibly can, even when all choices seem wrong.

We know that God causes everything to work together for the good of those who love God and are called according to his purpose for them.

ROMANS 8:28

GOING FURTHER

⊕ How do you decide what to do when there doesn't seem to be one "right" choice?

⊕ What decisions are you facing now? In what ways can you seek God's help to make the right choice?

⊕ How might God bring good out of difficult situations in your life?

⊕ What are you going to do about them?

THE WORD ON HARD CHOICES

Take some time to read one or more of the following Bible passages:

1 Kings 3:16-28; Daniel 6:1-16; Mark 12:13-17;
Luke 20:1-8; John 11:47-53; Romans 8:35-39

CHAPTER
TWELVE

HELP
UN-LOOKED
FOR

Just at that moment the Lord of the Eagles swept down from above, seized him in his talons, and was gone.

FROM CHAPTER SIX OF *The Hobbit*

It's three hours into *The Lord of the Rings: The Return of the King,* and the world is coming to an end on-screen. The movie theater is packed with fans who've waited years for this final installment of the blockbuster trilogy. Sitting with them are friends or family members who were dragged there by force. Only the really die-hard Tolkien junkies have any clue what's going to happen. The rest sit and gape and grip the edge of their seats.

On-screen, the good forces of Middle-earth are taking their last stand against Sauron. They're surrounded by masses of the enemy, squeezed by the sheer numbers crushing in around them (caught between the orcs and a hard place, you might say). Trolls sweep through the ranks, stomping and thrashing and moshing everything to bits. Little hobbits are among those fighting to give Frodo and Sam their last chance—a bit of time, a moment when the Great Eye of Sauron is distracted. But they are failing. The battle is hopeless. All seems lost. All *is* lost.

And then it comes: the unexpected. From a great distance, huge creatures appear in the sky, wheeling through the air as they did for Bilbo and Gandalf—not once, but twice—in the pages of *The Hobbit*. Gandalf glances up, surprised but not really surprised. A shout goes up, a cry of joy at the unforeseen: "The Eagles are coming! The Eagles are coming!"

While the Tolkien junkies give a noisy ovation, the rest of the moviegoers lean toward each other and holler, "The *what* are coming? Eagles? I don't remember anything about eagles. Did I miss something?"

Well, sort of. That is, we had a quick glimpse of an eagle coming to Gandalf's rescue way back in movie #1 when the wizard is trapped at the top of Saruman's tower. But other than that, the eagles don't play a leading role among the many characters in *The Lord of the Rings*. Their appearance is totally unexpected.

And in a way, that's exactly the point. Those who've read *The Hobbit* may recognize what's going on, but perhaps even they have forgotten what role the majestic birds have played before.

The first encounter takes place in chapter 6 of *The Hobbit*, when Bilbo, Gandalf, and the dwarves have escaped from goblins only to be caught by wolves. Just when Gandalf has decided there's nothing left to do but die a noble death, fighting as best he can, the eagles make a quick entrance into the story and save the day. Tolkien's readers are taken by surprise. Still later, when the Battle of Five Armies is beyond all hope of winning, the eagles make yet another entrance, and Bilbo is the first to cry out, "The Eagles! . . . The Eagles are coming!"[20] And though we've seen them before, they take us by surprise yet again. Then in *The Lord of the Rings* they show up a third, a fourth, even a fifth time. How many times must they appear before we finally begin to expect them?

Here Tolkien introduces yet another of his crucial themes: "help un-looked for." At the very moment when all seems lost, help arrives that we did not anticipate. Tolkien coined his own word for it: *eucatastrophe,* "the sudden happy turn in a story which pierces you with a joy that brings tears."[21] Instead of a catastrophe, when everything takes a turn for the worse, *eucatastrophe* is a turn for the better.

It's a theme born out of the Christian faith rather than a pagan understanding of the universe. Both views agree that we human beings are small, frail, and limited in our ability to battle the forces of the world that seek to destroy us. In response, the pagan worldview says, "We cannot win this on our own strength. Therefore, let us go down fighting nobly and die well." The Christian worldview, on the other hand, says, "We cannot win this on our own strength. Therefore, we must rely on a Power outside of ourselves to win this for us."

According to Tolkien, the coming of Jesus into our story was the *eucatastrophe* of history.[22] The human race was dying in sin, destroying itself. Then when we least expected it, God sent Jesus to save us from sin and death. As the apostle Paul wrote, "When we were utterly helpless, Christ came at just the right time and died for us sinners" (Romans 5:6). Help arrived when we had almost given up looking for it.

Jesus' followers regularly got a taste of this

"help un-looked for." In one incident, two sisters named Mary and Martha sent word to Jesus that their brother, Lazarus, had become ill. They waited and waited for Jesus to arrive, knowing he had the power to heal. But Jesus didn't come and he didn't come—not even at the last moment, right up to when Lazarus died. So they stopped looking. When Jesus finally showed up four days later, the funeral was already underway. "Lord," Mary said in her grief, "If you had been here, my brother would not have died" (John 11:32). It didn't occur to her to ask for help; it was all over, as far as she was concerned. Yet the Bible tells us that Jesus went to the tomb and commanded Lazarus to come out alive. Lazarus did, and the disciples and mourners got a taste of *eucatastrophe* on a personal level.

We all experience times in life when we need God's help. Perhaps we're facing a crucial decision. Or maybe we're not getting along with the boss or our financial-aid package doesn't come through like we expected. We spend months in prayer; we exercise patience; we scan the horizon, hoping that somehow, in some way, God will come to the rescue. But nothing happens. Finally, with a sense of pagan resignation, we cross over into the land beyond hope and cease looking for help altogether.

Yet that's exactly where God meets us.

Sometimes his help has been there all along, but we just didn't recognize it for what it was. Other times he sends people our way at exactly the right moment, including those from whom we'd rather not accept help. Whatever the case, God comes to us un-looked for, like the eagles in Tolkien's tales, and the trick is to recognize him even when we're no longer looking. Then we can lead others to do the same.

God is our refuge and strength, always ready to help in times of trouble.

PSALM 46:1

GOING FURTHER

⊕ What is something you need God's help
for right now?

⊕ How might God be helping you already, perhaps
in a way you've overlooked or failed to expect?

⊕ What can you say to people who have given up
on receiving God's help for their problems or
circumstances?

⊕ How might God be using you to help them?

⊕ What are you going to do about it?

THE WORD ON HELP
UN-LOOKED FOR

Take some time to read one or more of the following
Bible passages:

Psalm 33:13-22, 61:1-4, 121:1-8, and 124:1-8;
Isaiah 41:10; Matthew 24:43-44; 2 Corinthians 6:2

CHOOSE YOUR OWN ADVENTURE

"So cheer up Bilbo and don't look so glum. Cheer up Thorin and Company! This is your expedition after all."

GANDALF, CHAPTER SEVEN OF *The Hobbit*

We're now a third of the way through Bilbo's adventure, and to our relief, Bilbo, Gandalf, and the dwarves are safe for the meantime, rescued by the unexpected eagles. After a good sleep and a decent meal (their first for days and days), the company is transported to the outskirts of property belonging to a mysterious character named Beorn. Here Gandalf hopes they can find shelter and rest before the treacherous journey through Mirkwood. But before arriving at Beorn's house, Gandalf makes it clear to the company that he will not be traveling with them all the way to the Lonely Mountain.

The old disappearing trick again! Everyone is upset at this news. Won't Gandalf always be there for them? Won't he stick around to pull them out of scrapes and blunders and mishaps? No, he insists, "for after all this is not my adventure."[23] After a brief sojourn at Beorn's house, Gandalf takes them to the edge of Mirkwood Forest and there he leaves them, just as he said he would.

And now they're really on their own. Whatever happens from this point on, they can't count on Gandalf to get them out of trouble. They must choose their own adventure, for better or worse. It's *their* expedition, not his, though he's been the primary manager so far. Now it's their turn to face moments of decision, make choices, and live with the consequences.

In a strange sort of way, we can relate to their dismay at being turned out into the big, bad world on their own. During our infancy and childhood, most decisions are made for us. Our parents decided where we'd live, what we'd eat, what we'd wear, who we'd hang out with, and what activities we'd be involved in. But gradually they give us more and more say in those decisions until eventually we're called upon to make our own adult way in the world, even if we don't feel quite ready.

There are lots of conflicts at this stage. We slide back and forth between wanting more independence and wanting someone else to make the big decisions (especially the ones involving money we'd rather spend on fun stuff like a new stereo than on boring things like car insurance). Sometimes it feels like it would be easier to go back to the childhood stage. We are scared to make all these decisions. It's too much responsibility. We don't feel up to the task. Maybe we have a perfectionist streak that makes us afraid of messing up, which makes the whole experience even worse.

If we're honest, sometimes we wish God would treat us like puppets and simply move us where he wants us to go. It would be so much easier that way, right? "Lift your left hand, then your foot, now your right hand. Go to this college. Marry that person. Nod your head. Smile." But we are not marionettes controlled by some master puppeteer. Nor are we bound by fate to follow a certain path we can never stray from, no matter what we do. Instead, we are characters in a story in which the Author gives us freedom to make our own choices.

Yes, God has an overall plan for where he wants the broader story of human history to go; and yes, God has an overall plan for your life, too. And while he deeply desires for you to follow that plan—since it's designed with your very best in mind—he also respects your freedom to choose when and how you'll get there. He even respects your freedom to choose not to get there at all. It'd break his heart if you were to reject his plan, because he knows *your* heart eventually will be broken by your own mistakes, but he allows you to make those mistakes.

After all, this is not *his* adventure. He's not conducting some grand experiment to see how these human rats will perform, nor is he manipulating operations to make himself look good. One of the reasons for the adventure of your life and faith is that God delights in you and in the development of your character. He's like an author who deeply loves his characters and is fascinated and delighted (and sometimes appalled) by the things they do and say. He's also like a parent who is eternally attentive to his children but knows they must forge their own paths in this world if they are to be strong, wise, and unique. He made you to be your own person. You must choose your own adventure.

Jesus took a similar attitude toward his disciples when his time on earth was drawing to a close. He insisted that he must go away—and the disciples would not be able to follow him . . . yet. They were bewildered: "Lord, where are you going?" Peter asked (John 13:36). "You can't go with me now," Jesus replied. He promised to return briefly, after his resurrection from death, but then he would "go to the Father" (14:28), and the disciples would be on their own in the world.

It's not hard to imagine the sudden panic they felt at his words. "But what will we do without you? How will we survive? Who will tell us what to do and where to go? But . . . but . . ." Jesus was quick to reassure them that they won't be utterly alone; the Holy Spirit would be with them to comfort, empower, and guide. He also offered a host of instructions for how to live as his disciples after he was gone, sort of like handing them a map and compass and saying, "Go that way." Even though this was not *his* adventure, he didn't leave them stranded.

And he doesn't leave us stranded either. We too

have the Holy Spirit, who gives us the power to do the right thing. We too have his instructions, written in the Bible like sticky-note reminders. When facing unknown adventures lurking beyond the horizon, we can take heart in a God who sees us as unique characters in his story. Guided by the Holy Spirit and by Jesus' instructions, we can enter the next stage of the journey with confidence, keeping our eyes fixed on the reward that lies ahead.

As Gandalf said to Bilbo and the dwarves, "Think of the treasure at the end, and forget the forest and the dragon, at any rate until tomorrow morning!"[24]

Don't be troubled. You trust God, now trust in me.

JOHN 14:1

GOING FURTHER

⊕ Why doesn't God simply move you where he wants you to go? What does that tell you about him? What does that tell you about yourself?

⊕ How easy or difficult is it for you to make decisions?

⊕ Do you generally prefer help, or would you rather plunge ahead and decide on your own?

⊕ What are some of the decisions you are facing right now?

⊕ How can you discern which choices God wants you to make?

⊕ What are you going to do about it?

THE WORD ON CHOOSING YOUR OWN ADVENTURE

Take some time to read one or more of the following Bible passages:

Deuteronomy 30:15-20; Joshua 24:15; Psalm 119:26-32; Proverbs 19:3; John 14:15-21

CHAPTER FOURTEEN

STICK TO THE PATH!

"Good-bye! Be good, take care of yourselves—
and DON'T LEAVE THE PATH!"

GANDALF, CHAPTER SEVEN OF *The Hobbit*

Gandalf has said he won't be with Bilbo and
the dwarves on this stage of the journey, but
he isn't about to leave them in the middle of
nowhere without *something* to hold on to. He
and Beorn have brought them safely to the edge
of Mirkwood Forest and pointed them in the

direction they are to go. But there's one more thing. Gandalf has given very clear instructions, repeated numerous times and with great urgency:

STICK TO THE PATH.

There's only one safe passage through the treacherous forest of Mirkwood, and that's the track cutting right through the middle. If the dwarves' mission is to be successful, they must do exactly as Gandalf says. But of course they do leave the path, and no one is surprised when bad things happen as a result.

To be fair, it's not that the dwarves *want* to get off track. In fact, they have every good intention of obeying Gandalf's instructions. But the monotony of their situation—hiking the same trail through endless trees, day after day— combined with their gradual descent into near starvation, sets the stage for a misadventure that has the power to sabotage the mission altogether.

There are several aspects of their experience

that have implications for the journey of faith. First, we find an important distinction between *adventure* and *misadventure*. Adventures are what happen when we're on the right road. There will be hardships and difficulties that God allows (and designs!) to test and strengthen our character. But if we wander off the appointed track, we set ourselves up for *misadventures*—bad events and poor choices that have the power to derail us from completing the journey altogether. Clearly, adventures are a good thing; misadventures are not.

Second, as we've discussed in previous chapters, encountering the unpredictable is all part of the adventure. But so is enduring the *predictable*, day after day after day. Bilbo and the dwarves wake up every morning to see the same thing they did yesterday and will see again tomorrow: nothing but trees for miles. Not only that but they face the same task for today that they did yesterday and will face again tomorrow: take the forest track and stick with it. There's no way out of it, no possibility of breaking the monotony of their routine. If they wish to accomplish the mission, there will be a boring predictability to each day and the next and the next, until they wonder if they're going mad.

The same can be true with the adventure of faith. Sometimes there's just no adventure at all. Sometimes you wake up in the morning and—unless there's a cataclysmic disaster or even just the slightest deviation from the norm—the day's events will go exactly as predicted, with no change from the everyday tasks God has called you to do. Homework is still homework, laundry is still laundry, and dinner must be prepared before the end of the day. Even our times of prayer and devotion change little throughout the week, if we get up the energy to do them. The truth is, if we stick to the path God has chosen for us, we're not guaranteed eye-popping, jaw-dropping, heart-racing adventures all the time. In fact, we may be asked to do the mundane, the banal, the mind-numbingly boring.

And that's exactly when we're tempted to stray. We begin to starve for change, for something to break the tedium of our days, to get the heart rate up again. So we contemplate taking the slightest jog off the track, just to see what's out there. Those are the times when the misadventures of our lost and wandering peers look almost tempting. "Why shouldn't I party just this once? Why shouldn't I skip this assignment or spend my money on a new outfit instead of the mission fund-raiser? Why not ignore the needs of my elderly neighbor, just for this week?" We begin to wonder if there's perhaps some other path.

Other times, we're tempted to stray because we have genuine needs that must be met, like the starving dwarves in Bilbo's tale. Perhaps we're simply exhausted at the end of the day and need to relax. Why not with a six-pack? Or maybe we feel the pain of poor self-esteem. Why not pick on someone else in an attempt to feel good at another's expense? If we're not careful, our genuine needs can lead us to justify all sorts of unhealthy behavior.

Through the treacherous landscape of sin, God has mapped out the way of righteousness and instructs us to walk in it. "Be good," we hear him saying throughout the pages of the Bible: "Take care of yourself. And stick to the path!" The point of the path is not somehow to lead us away from what the world calls fun, but to help us survive life itself with our dignity intact and to enable us to accomplish the mission.

But we're not left to do this on our own. God sent Jesus, not only to be our guide and leader, but to be the path itself. Jesus told his disciples both "Follow me" (Mark 8:34) *and* "I am the way" (John 14:6). He led Peter, Andrew, John, and the others on a path of right thinking and right doing that changed the world—with himself as both the example and the trail. As they quickly learned, there are no other roads to the ultimate destination of God's presence

and peace. Jesus is it. Everything else leads to
misadventure, to danger, and even to failure.

So we make the decision to walk with Jesus.
We expect adventures: to serve on mission trips,
to give when we really can't afford to, to open
our home to the homeless. We're up for the
challenge of visiting inmates in prison or working a second job to help support a missionary
or taking meals to folks recovering from surgery.
What we don't expect, however, is the sheer
tedium of sticking to this path of righteousness
day after day after day. We're unprepared for
the temptation to wander until we're already off
the trail.

Ultimately, however, we are not left to our
own devices. We learn that good can come out
of our misadventures. As Bilbo and the dwarves
eventually discovered, their circuitous route
off the beaten path proved to be the only way
through Mirkwood. They could not have fore-
seen it, nor could they use it to excuse their
behavior. Neither can we. God chooses to act

on our behalf, despite our wanderings, and
he will put us on the right path again—if we'll
let him!

*The highway to hell is broad, and its gate is wide for the
many who choose the easy way. But the gateway to life is
small, and the road is narrow, and only a few ever find it.*

MATTHEW 7:13-14

GOING FURTHER

⊕ How do you know when you're on the path God
intends for you?

⊕ How do you know when you've wandered away
from God's path? How do you get back on it again?

⊕ How can you encourage those who've wandered
from God's path to walk with Jesus again?

⊕ What inspires you to stick to the path of righteousness, even when it feels monotonous or boring
at times?

⊕ What are you going to do when you're tempted
to stray?

THE WORD ON STICKING
TO THE PATH

Take some time to read one or more of the following
proverbs:

Proverbs 3:5-8, 4:10-27, 10:17, 16:17, 16:25, and 22:6

CHAPTER
FIFTEEN

THE UNLIKELY HERO

*Somehow the killing of the giant spider, all alone by himself
in the dark without the help of the wizard or the dwarves
or of anyone else, made a great difference to Mr. Baggins.*

FROM CHAPTER EIGHT OF *The Hobbit*

Perhaps one of the greatest strengths of Tolkien's heroes is their very ordinariness. Hobbits are not comic-book superpowers, endowed with extraordinary abilities from accidental chemical mutations. Nor are they patterned after the mighty warrior-kings of ancient Norse mythology, which

Tolkien knew so well. No, they are an utterly unique invention: quiet, average folk from a quiet, average land, virtually unknown by the powerful rulers of Tolkien's imaginary world.

Gandalf is the first to guess that these unassuming folk have hidden strengths and can be "as fierce as a dragon in a pinch"[25]—though it takes a great many chapters in *The Hobbit* before he's proven right. In fact, for the first 150 pages or so, even *we* begin to wonder if Gandalf made the right choice. Bilbo seems more of a burden than a blessing to the company of dwarves and is even sometimes downright annoying. Then suddenly, just when we're tempted to holler, "Quit whining!" and throw the book across the room, Bilbo does something really heroic and totally unexpected—something that surprises even himself.

The mishap in Mirkwood is not the only time Bilbo becomes lost and separated from the others. The first was in the goblin tunnels in the Misty Mountains. Now he's in the treacherous forest, and this time Gandalf isn't around to come to the rescue. When the hobbit finds himself trapped in deadly threads from a giant spider, he must act quickly. There's no time to think. Our unlikely hero cuts his way free and then turns his little sword on the spider itself. Then, with his newfound confidence, he goes on to free the dwarves from a decidedly sticky situation.

While Bilbo may not be endowed with extraordinary abilities, he has the good sense to make use of whatever talents and resources he has at his disposal. For resources he has the Ring, which renders him invisible, and his sword, which has something of a personal vendetta against evil creatures of any kind. For talents he has the ability of his race to walk in utter silence, as well as fairly decent aim—not to mention his knack for making up rhymes and riddles on the spot. In short, though Bilbo is an unlikely hero, he is exactly the right guy for this particular situation.

It's a theme we find comforting, isn't it? In a video-game world of action-adventure sequences and heroes with bulging biceps, it's a relief to find a leading character who is pretty much ordinary. There are no rippling muscles, no impossible stunts, no machismo or bravado with Bilbo. This is a fellow to whom we can actually relate.

And so are the disciples in the great Christian story. We've already said that these were not the most obvious heroes God could have selected for the adventure with Jesus. Yet even the disciples themselves had a hard time accepting the fact that Jesus, the long-awaited Messiah, had not been born in a household of wealth, the child of some leading priest or other powerful figure. Instead he was born in a tiny suburb of Jerusalem and raised in the rural town of Nazareth, a redneck by the standards of the day. In fact, when told about Jesus and where he was from, a man named Nathanael—who would eventually become one of the twelve disciples—said, "Nazareth! . . . Can anything good come from there?" (John 1:46).

Even after weeks and months and years on the road with Jesus, the disciples still didn't get it. They often were taken by surprise at the various people Jesus honored with heroic tasks, despite the fact that the disciples themselves were unlikely heroes for the adventure of faith. Take the little boy who offered his five loaves and two fish for the feeding of the five thousand, as recorded in John 6. It probably didn't even occur to the disciples to consider the boy's gifts until their situation became desperate. Otherwise, they might have overlooked him altogether.

And we can't forget the parable of the Good Samaritan in Luke 10:30-37. In that tale, Jesus chose to honor one of the most hated people groups in the region by giving them the role of hero—a lesson to all of his hearers about the grace of God. Jesus was essentially saying that the God of the universe chooses the least likely to come to the rescue of those in need. God will even choose *you*.

You may not have extraordinary abilities,
but you've been given resources and talents
that God wants to use for heroic tasks. Think
of the unlikely heroes you've met in your own
life—ordinary folks who've stepped up to the
plate when others needed help. There's the lady
at church who visits the elderly every week.
Or the teenager who organizes free babysitting
for a young widower. Or the mentor who goes
to schools and spends time with troubled kids.
Everywhere you look, there are people sacrificing
time, money, and energy to be the kind of heroes
God calls us to be.

So how can *you* be an unlikely hero in your
own community? The list of prayer requests
in your church bulletin is a great place to start.
You might even talk with your pastor or student
director about specific needs in the church that
you might be able to fill. Spend time in prayer,
asking God's guidance for how and where to
serve. Then do it.

It's possible you're already neck-deep in semi-heroic responsibilities. In fact, some of you probably have overcommitted yourselves, hoping you can be a spiritual superpower. Caffeine helps feed the illusion, of course, but sooner or later you'll discover problems you're simply not gifted to face, circumstances beyond your strengths or abilities. And that's okay. Through the process of prayer and discernment, God will show you where to concentrate your energies for maximum effectiveness.

God has called you on this adventure of faith to serve a specific purpose, just as Gandalf chose Bilbo for the expedition to the Lonely Mountain. As the wizard sternly told the dwarves, "I brought him, and I don't bring things that are of no use."[26] What use will you be?

So, my dear brothers and sisters, be strong and steady, always enthusiastic about the Lord's work, for you know that nothing you do for the Lord is ever useless.

1 CORINTHIANS 15:58

GOING FURTHER

⊕ What resources has God given you (time, money, stuff) to help others? How about your talents—what are you good at? How can God use those talents?

⊕ How can you be a blessing rather than a burden to the people in your life?

⊕ Who are the unlikely heroes in your church or community? What do you admire most about them? How can you emulate their lives of service?

⊕ What are the needs in your community?

⊕ What are you going to do about those needs?

THE WORD ON UNLIKELY HEROES

Take some time to read one or more of the following Bible passages:

Judges 6:11-16; Matthew 13:53-58; Mark 12:41-44; John 6:3-13 and 7:40-52; Galatians 1:13-16

CHAPTER
SIXTEEN

GOOD LUCK?

Luck of an unusual kind was with Bilbo then.

FROM CHAPTER NINE OF *The Hobbit*

For an interesting exercise, skim through the pages of *The Hobbit* and *The Lord of the Rings* and count how many times the word *luck* appears. The most obvious reference, of course, is to the "unlucky" number of dwarves who arrive on Bilbo's doorstep in the opening chapter of *The Hobbit*. This is in part why they ask Gandalf to find one more member for their expedition.

As the story progresses, we observe that Bilbo himself sets good store by luck, considering events to be lucky or unlucky, depending on the situation. He's a fairly uncomplicated hobbit with a simple view of things. No introspective philosophizing about some higher power for Bilbo! As he says to Frodo before the younger hobbit leaves for Mordor, "Good . . . good luck!"[27]—a humorous understatement, as Tolkien probably intended. (Frodo doesn't need luck; he needs a miracle!) Bilbo survives his own adventure by what he calls good luck, yet along the way we sense that something more is going on.

Take, for example, his sudden opportunity to help the dwarves escape from the Elvenking's palace after their nearly disastrous misadventure in Mirkwood. By "chance," he discovers that empty barrels are regularly sent down a hatch into the river and then downstream to the Long Lake. Soon the opportunity arises to grab the keys, release the dwarves from prison, and seal them in barrels for the journey. "Luck of an unusual kind was with Bilbo then," Tolkien writes in chapter 9. And we can't help wondering, *Is it really luck that Tolkien has in mind, or is it something else?*

What is luck, anyway? We toss the word around lightly, saying "Good luck!" in a cheerful voice to friends facing final exams. But what do we mean by that? Generally speaking, we mean that we hope events fall in their favor. We hope they remember the right answers at the right time and pass with flying colors. With good luck, things turn out to our advantage; we succeed at what we try. With bad luck, events turn against us and we fail.

We use the word "chance" in a similar way: "By chance, I just *happened* to see her out of the corner of my eye." Today we use the term in a fairly impersonal way to refer to what seem like random events—the natural result, statistically speaking, of being in the right place at the right time. But in ancient pagan times, people believed that luck and chance were guided by certain powers. Those powers either favored you or they didn't; you were either born lucky (favored) or you weren't. Sometimes your luck could turn; you might have a string of unsuccessful events and then suddenly succeed. All of this, in the ancient worldview, was because "Lady Luck" or some other power was with you.

When it comes to Tolkien's references to luck throughout *The Hobbit*, we sense he's using the term according to this older meaning rather than our contemporary definition. Bilbo's luck is of "an unusual kind." He is favored, you might say. Clearly, something more than random chance is guiding Bilbo's adventure, as Gandalf hints in the book's closing pages. Bilbo is more than merely lucky; he's in good hands.

We've already discussed the fact that behind every good adventure story is an overall plan, supervised by the story's author. We've explored the implications of this plan for our own adventure of faith with God. Beyond that, we've dived into the concept of our unique *chosen-ness:* that God has specifically favored us for this adventure. So why is it that our plans fail sometimes, when other people—who aren't walking with God, as far as we can tell—seem to succeed at whatever they do? Why do they have all the "luck" and we don't?

It's not that God plays favorites. He doesn't help certain people succeed while setting the rest up for failure. For some reason unknown to us, he does allow a significant amount of worldly success—or what some call good luck—to those who don't deserve it, and he also allows a bewildering amount of failure, or bad luck, to those who don't really deserve it either. As the writer of Ecclesiastes wrote several thousand years ago, "Even though the actions of godly and wise people are in God's hands, no one knows whether or not God will show them favor in this life" (9:1).

At the same time, God does choose certain people to perform specific tasks that need doing, and for whatever reason, those people are in the right position at the right time. Like Mary, the mother of Jesus, or Paul, the first missionary, they display a certain readiness or availability, along with the gifts and talents required. Besides that, they're not interested in taking all the glory for themselves. They know when to say, "That was well done, but it really had very little to do with me, in the end."

The disciples were people like that. They were hand-selected by Jesus to walk with him and then appointed to spread the gospel to the whole world. But even though at various times they probably felt pretty "lucky," their favored-ness didn't lead to riches or worldly success. Jesus could feed five thousand people with just a few loaves and fish, but he didn't use his power to buy a condo in Cancun for himself and the guys. Instead, they remained homeless and hungry most of the time.

In fact, all who follow Jesus will face at some point what feels like stroke after stroke of bad luck. We're not exempt from losing our wallets, blowing a tire, or returning from spring break to discover that someone has broken into our apartment. On top of that, we'll experience tough situations that are directly connected to our decision to follow Jesus, such as a budget stretched thin because we're helping those in need. But at other times we'll experience the sudden buoyancy that comes from having God on our side, blessing us in ways we couldn't have dreamed or imagined. When God has chosen us to do his work, the doors will open eventually.

So there's really no such thing as luck, not even in Bilbo's story. As Gandalf tells him, "You don't really suppose, do you, that all your adventures and escapes were managed by mere luck, just for your sole benefit?"[28]

*We may throw the dice, but the L*ORD* determines how they fall.*

PROVERBS 16:33

GOING FURTHER

● What do you mean when you tell someone "Good luck"?

● Why is there no such thing as luck or chance, from God's perspective?

● How do you interact with God when you have a bunch of "bad luck" all at once?

● How do you respond when someone complains that God is unfair?

● What if circumstances truly are unfair for that person? What are you going to do about it?

THE WORD ON GOD'S FAVOR

Take some time to read one or more of the following Bible passages:

Genesis 39:1-6; Proverbs 11:27; Ecclesiastes 9:11; Luke 1:26-28; Galatians 2:6

DECENT
COMPANIONS

*There it is: dwarves are not heroes . . . but are decent enough
people like Thorin and Company, if you don't expect too much.*

FROM CHAPTER TWELVE OF *The Hobbit*

It's the annual family reunion at Hicksville
Central Campground, and somehow you've been
dragged along *again*. There's Aunt Edith, sweating
in a bright purple jumpsuit as she dishes out the
tuna casserole to Aunt Agnes, with whom she's
already arguing. And there's your socially inept

cousin, Junior, who latches onto you as his unwilling partner in the three-legged race. Then a firm hand grasps your shoulder, and you turn to see Uncle Billy, a simply enormous man in a checked grilling apron. "Son," he says, "I need you at the grill." Great. There's no escaping now.

Four hours in the blazing heat, dishing out gross hot dogs to bickering, annoying people . . . it's enough to make you give up in protest. *If I weren't such a decent guy,* you tell yourself, *I would have ditched this crew a long time ago.* Yet there it is: You *are* a decent guy. This is your family, for better or worse. And there's nothing you can do about it.

By the middle of the expedition to the Lonely Mountain, poor Bilbo—the most decent of decent guys—has had about as much of his fellow adventurers as he can stand. It starts right at the beginning, when they march through his front door expecting to be fed and housed at his expense. "Confusticate and bebother these dwarves!" Bilbo says to himself. "Why don't they come and lend a hand?"[29] Chapter after chapter, they continue to treat him like some lower-class citizen who has been hired to do the dirty work, especially when someone is needed to scout out potentially dangerous situations.

We don't see Bilbo standing up for himself until he has spent more than a week sneaking around the Elvenking's palace, trying to find a way for the dwarves to escape. He's there for *their* sakes, anyway, so when they balk at his plan to seal them in barrels, he's annoyed enough to suggest that they go back to prison then and come up with a better idea. And finally, when they arrive bruised and battered upon the shores of the Long Lake, expressing their irritation with Bilbo once again, he doesn't even try to be kind in response.

Yet these are his traveling companions, for better or worse. Gandalf has selected them for the journey. If at times Bilbo doesn't much like them, there's nothing he can do about it now. He and the dwarves must offer each other whatever respect and tolerance they can manage if they wish to accomplish the mission. And because Bilbo is a decent fellow, he's determined to give it a try. What else can he do?

There's perhaps nothing that tests our character more than getting along with our companions on this journey of life and faith. Just one family reunion is all it takes to point out our weaknesses. We may love these people, yes, due to some trace of clan loyalty still alive in our genes. But do we *like* them? Are they the kind of people we wish to hang out with? Are they our heroes? Maybe so; maybe not. Sometimes it's about all we can do to offer them a civil word.

Most family tensions center on domestic duties. Someone has to cook, clean, do the laundry, scrub the toilet bowl, pick up more milk, drop so-and-so off at such-and-such place; and it's only fair that everyone take a turn. You may get annoyed when those in charge assign you jobs you don't like. And you probably get even more annoyed when the assignments keep coming. Just when you've finished loading the dishwasher, for example, the family drill sergeant hands you a gas can and points to the lawn mower. Conflagration, anyone?

The same is often true in the family of faith, especially when it comes to a local church with a budget, building, programs, and staff. It takes work to keep a nonprofit organization going, particularly if that organization is focused on reaching out to its local community. Meals must be delivered, financial decisions made, ten-year goals set, staff members paid, children taught, mission trips organized, and siding replaced. People have to get along and do their part if the overall mission is to be accomplished.

Chances are, if you're involved at all, you're involved in too much. That's because somewhere down the line someone isn't picking up the slack. And because you're a decent person, you soon find yourself slogging away in the church kitchen, thinking to yourself, *Confusticate and bebother these people! Why don't they lend a hand?* It's enough to make any adventurer walk away in disgust, wondering if this faith thing is really worth it.

We're not the first people to experience these tensions. Thumbing through the pages of the Gospels, we soon come across Mary and her sister, Martha, again—only this time they're hosting a party, not a funeral. Jesus is there, along with the disciples and other stragglers, which makes quite a crowd. In the days before kitchen appliances, feeding such a crew would take more than one willing pair of hands. But Martha soon discovers she's the only one in the kitchen while Mary is out there listening to Jesus. Frustrated, Martha goes straight to him: "Lord, doesn't it seem unfair to you that my sister just sits here while I do all the work? Tell her to come and help me" (Luke 10:40). But Jesus refuses. What Mary is doing is even more important than dinner, he insists, "and I won't take it away from her" (11:42). We can assume they all had dinner that night anyway, but when and how is left up to the imagination.

While you may feel like indentured servant-hood is *not* what you signed up for in following Jesus, God has different plans. We are called to love those whom he's given us as fellow travelers on the journey—and not only to love them, but to serve them as well. There's no greater test of our character than when we're up to our elbows in greasy suds, picking up the slack for some brother or sister who gets on our nerves—or cleaning up after fellow believers who've failed to say thank you.

Yet these are the people God has given you: your spiritual brothers and sisters. This is your family of faith. You can't just walk away without uprooting your spiritual life and sabotaging the mission God has called all of you on together.

Things could be worse. These traveling companions of yours are not heroes, but they are decent people, though you must learn not to expect too much at first. Never forget that we all have a lot of growing up to do, and your fellow travelers will need to offer *you* patience and grace before the end. Will they, like the dwarves with Bilbo, be glad they brought you along?

> *I command you to love each other in the same way that I love you. And here is how to measure it— the greatest love is shown when people lay down their lives for their friends.*

JOHN 15:12-13

GOING FURTHER

⊕ Who among your family and friends are your heroes? Why?

⊕ When is it difficult for you to get along with friends or family? In all honesty, how patient are you?

⊕ When are you difficult to get along with?

⊕ How does God want you to treat the people who annoy you?

⊕ What are you going to do about it?

THE WORD ON GETTING ALONG

Take some time to read one or more of the following
Bible passages:

Genesis 37:1-4 and 45:12-15; Exodus 17:1-7;
Matthew 5:38-42; Luke 6:37-38; Romans 15:5;
Colossians 3:12-15; 1 John 4:20-21

CHAPTER EIGHTEEN

LIVING LEGENDS

"I am Thorin son of Thrain son of Thror King under the Mountain! I return!"

THORIN, CHAPTER TEN OF *The Hobbit*

Surprise! Aragorn isn't the first king to "return" in Tolkien's tales of Middle-earth.

In chapter 10 of *The Hobbit*, we learn that old stories and songs have long prophesied the return of the King under the Mountain, though for the people of Lake Town, as Tolkien says, "this pleasant legend did not much affect their daily business."[30] Upon Thorin's arrival by barrel to the shores of the lake, he wastes no time in entering the town and declaring just exactly who he is. And the effect is tremendous. Within minutes, the townspeople are celebrating the fulfillment of all the old tales, throwing a party for the newly returned king.

Yet lurking in the background is the Master of the town. According to Tolkien, the man is decidedly unhappy to see the dwarves, though he hides his skepticism from the people out of fear they will turn on him. Inwardly, he not only refuses to believe that Thorin is who he says he is, but we learn that he never believed the prophecies in the first place. Besides that, Thorin's presence is a threat to the Master's position of power and authority. Tolkien spends few words on this character, but we get the impression he is highly critical of the Master's attitude of unbelief.

Skeptics abound in *The Lord of the Rings* as well.

Before he claims the throne, Aragorn, the long-awaited king of Gondor, slowly begins to test the waters of belief among ordinary folks in places like Rohan. When the Riders of Rohan come upon him and question his identity in the pages of *The Two Towers*, he boldly announces his name and lineage. This prompts a response of astonishment from the Riders, one of whom exclaims, "Do we walk in legends or on the green earth in the daylight?" Aragorn replies with what could be considered one of Tolkien's most intriguing statements in all of *The Lord of the Rings*: "A man may do both."[31]

A man may do both. In other words, just because something is labeled a *legend* doesn't mean it can't also be *fact*. There is such a thing as a *living legend*, when the stuff of stories comes crashing into the timeline of history as a datable event. It was an important theme for Tolkien's Christian faith and one that had profound impact on his friendship with C. S. Lewis.

Lewis, once an avowed atheist, had trouble

believing Christianity was anything more than just another myth—a lovely, wonderful story, to be sure, but just a story. It was Tolkien and one of his friends[32] who challenged Lewis to consider if perhaps a story could be both myth and fact at the same time. Christianity, they argued, is exactly that: the "True Myth." The stuff of legends became history in the person and work of Jesus Christ, and that's why Christianity is so compelling. That's why so many people have accepted Jesus' claims to the kingship of the universe—and of our hearts. In Christianity, as Tolkien put it, "Legend and History have met and fused."[33]

It was a powerful idea Lewis had never considered before. And yet the more he considered it, the more he realized it was probably, unbelievably, wonderfully true.

In a sense, the same challenge is put before us as Tolkien's readers. It's a challenge that first appears in the pages of *The Hobbit*, but takes on breadth and depth throughout *The Lord of the Rings*, culminating in Aragorn's crowning in Gondor

in *The Return of the King.* The challenge is twofold:
(1) Will we believe the old songs and stories
and legends about the return of *our* King? And
(2) will we recognize the moment when legend
becomes historical fact?

The people of Jesus' day faced those same
questions when he appeared on the scene. For
many long centuries, the nation of Israel had
been hoping and waiting for a descendent of
King David to sack their enemies and reclaim
the throne. Songs and stories throughout the
Old Testament prophesied that such a king
would return someday. So when Jesus was born,
holy prophets like Anna and Simeon and ordinary folks like Mary and the shepherds were
quick to recognize what was going on. The hero
of the old tales had been born in their midst.
The King had returned!

The disciples, too, were quick to identify
the kingship of Jesus, though many times they
mistook his true aims. Right up to his death,
they still assumed he would take up weapons

and fight the Romans—not realizing that he had come to conquer more powerful enemies than human rulers. As Jesus rode into Jerusalem in what would become the last week of his life, the disciples began to chant and sing the old prophesies, hailing the return of the King. Soon the people joined in, hosting an impromptu parade, despite the skepticism and outright disapproval of their leaders.

While Jesus didn't end up conquering the Romans, as his followers had hoped, he proved his role as King of the universe by conquering sin and death—the two greatest enemies of the human race. And since the days of his resurrection and ascension about two thousand years ago, his people have continued to create songs and stories and prophecies about his eventual return. Someday Jesus will come back, and this time he will claim the throne of the world and rule over a kingdom of peace for all eternity. As the disciple John prophesied in Revelation 11:15, "The whole world has now become the kingdom of our Lord and of his Christ, and he will reign forever and ever."

These are the stories and songs, tales and legends of our time. Do we believe them? Will we recognize Jesus when we see him? Will we be first, rather than last, to celebrate the return of the King?

But most important, will we allow this "pleasant legend" to affect our daily business? Will we live as people who acknowledge Christ's kingship and do his kingdom work until he returns?

If a person is ashamed of me and my message, I, the Son of Man, will be ashamed of that person when I return in my glory and in the glory of the Father and the holy angels.

LUKE 9:26

GOING FURTHER

⊕ Who among your friends is like C. S. Lewis before he converted to Christianity? What arguments does

your friend use against believing in Jesus? What
defense can you give for your faith?

⊕ How comfortable are you with what the Bible
says about the kingship and return of Jesus?

⊕ How much do the stories of Christ's return affect
your daily business?

⊕ What are you going to do about it?

THE WORD ON THE RETURN OF THE KING

Take some time to read one or more of the following
Bible passages:

Isaiah 9:6-7; Micah 1:3 and 5:2; Zechariah 9:9-10;
Matthew 24:30-35 and 25:13; Luke 17:20-24;
John 18:33-37; 2 Peter 3:8-10; Revelation 22:12

TRUE IDENTITY

Already he was a very different hobbit from the one that had run out without a pocket-handkerchief from Bag-End long ago.

FROM CHAPTER TWELVE OF *The Hobbit*

Finally, finally, after a nice little vacation in Lake Town, the dwarves and Bilbo arrive at their destination, the Lonely Mountain, where Smaug the dragon dwells. And now it's Bilbo's time to shine. Now the dwarves call upon him to fulfill the role he was drafted for in the first place, the "chosen and selected burglar"—as if he hasn't done enough for them already!

Tolkien tells us that Bilbo has begun to be the "real leader in their adventure," as in time the dwarves have come to rely on the hobbit for original ideas and bold actions. And now as they face the tunnels leading down to the dragon's lair, they send Bilbo first, ostensibly to scout things out, but in reality because they're too scared to go themselves. The dragon is asleep, to Bilbo's relief, giving the hobbit a chance to fulfill his role as official burglar. He steals a cup, Smaug awakes, and the game is up.

Well, almost. There's one more confrontation between Bilbo and Smaug, one that shows us just how much our hero has changed and grown since he left Bag-End all those months ago.

It's another Riddle Game, you might say, in the dark under a mountain. Except this time Bilbo faces off with a notorious dragon rather than an unknown creature called Gollum. Now the stakes are higher: Smaug is not to be bargained with. Yet despite Smaug's "overwhelming personality," Bilbo is able to keep his head rela-

tively clear and his dialogue sufficiently witty
before escaping just in time from the dragon's
fire. If it weren't for Smaug's rage and subsequent
destruction of the dwarves' secret door—leaving
them no way of escape—you might say that Bilbo
is the winner.

Yes, he has become "a very different hobbit"
indeed. But just because he's changed doesn't
mean he's lost all perspective on his true identity
as Bilbo Baggins of the Shire. It's not that he has
become something *other* than his true character;
it's that he has become the hobbit he was always
meant to be. Not something *less*, something *more*.
More of the adventurous Took that was already
in him, Gandalf might say, and not as much
Baggins.

Now Bilbo is no longer *pretending* to be an
"expert burglar," like a small child lugging
around his daddy's briefcase on an imaginary trip
to the office. Bilbo *is* an expert burglar. By steal-
ing the cup from Smaug's hoard while the dragon
is asleep, Bilbo becomes the thief he was hired to

be (albeit, as he says, "an honest one"[34]). He takes on the role Gandalf gave him from the beginning, a role that at first didn't seem like a very good fit. What Gandalf saw in Bilbo, back before the whole adventure started, was Bilbo's true character—not some twisted distortion of reality—and all that was needed were the trials and challenges of the adventure to bring it out.

The disciple Peter understood this kind of transformation well (though God never calls anyone to burglary!). Peter's given name, before Jesus came along, was Simon. Then one day he made a strong statement of faith about who Jesus really was (see Matthew 16:13-18), and Jesus declared Simon's new name to be Peter, which means "rock" (*petra* in Latin, which is why we refer to things that have become rocks as *petrified*). But it was a good long while before Simon Peter became the spiritual "rock" he was meant to be. In fact, on the night Jesus was arrested, Peter fled for his life with the other disciples. Things looked a little more hopeful when Peter showed up in the crowd at the courtyard where Jesus was tied up as a prisoner; but soon Peter's courage failed, and he denied three times that he had ever known Jesus. So much for rock-solid faith!

It wasn't until after Jesus' death, resurrection, and return to heaven—when the disciples were on their own with no Savior to lead them in tough times—that Peter became the "rock." Empowered by the Holy Spirit, he stood up in front of a crowd of thousands in Jerusalem and preached the Good News about Jesus (see Acts 2). Once he started delivering this bold message, he didn't stop. He took the Good News even to the non-Jews in different cities in the surrounding lands, facing beatings, imprisonment, and eventually execution. But along the way, something in him changed from his old "Simon" days. He became "Peter" in more than name only: He *was* the rock.

God sends us on the adventure of faith in part for us to discover who we really are. Along the way, our true strengths (and weaknesses) are revealed, along with our unique gifts and talents. More important, we discover just how God wants us to use those gifts to pursue the purpose and vocation he has had in mind for us all the time. In this way, our lives no longer point inward, at ourselves, but outward, giving God the glory.

The primary goal is to become more like Jesus. That's the whole purpose of this faith adventure: transformation—not becoming something *less* than we are, a pale shadow of our former selves, but becoming something *more* than we could ever become on our own. We surrender our old selves and take on a new "self," one that is more like Jesus: our Captain, the One who sent us on this journey. We no longer usurp his well-deserved starring role but surrender center stage to him.

Now, at first the idea sounds scary. We have this freaky, ridiculous notion—probably from watching too many *X-Files* episodes—that in surrendering ourselves to Christ we're going to become possessed by some long-dead personality and start channeling his voice, or we'll be brainwashed and drink poisoned Slurpees or something. At the very least, we worry that we're going to lose our uniqueness, that we'll become like all the other "Christians" out there, whatever that means, a great homogenous mass of drooling bores—or so the world tells us.

But in fact, the opposite is true. When we surrender our very selves to Christ and embark on the adventure of faith, we become more the unique person we were always created to be, not less. Popular culture sells a different story, one that too many of us believe: "Cut yourself off from your family, your past, your faith, whatever has been holding you back, and you'll finally be free to 'be yourself.'" If we buy the lie, sooner or later we realize we've been put in greater bondage to conformity than ever, having become so much like the unhappy, money-hungry, self-obsessed people around us that we can hardly tell where their lives end and ours begin. Not only that but we've cut ourselves off from the very source of our true identity. We no longer know who we are.

It's one of the great paradoxes of faith, a seemingly counterintuitive truth that we understand only once we've given it a shot: When we surrender our false identity to God—the identity we've allowed the world to give us—he gives us a new identity that is more truly who we really are, who we were always meant to be. And through the challenges and trials of this faith adventure, that's what we ultimately become: our true selves.

As Gandalf says, with his wry sense of humor, "My dear Bilbo! Something is the matter with you! You are not the hobbit that you were."[35]

What this means is that those who become Christians become new persons. They are not the same anymore, for the old life is gone. A new life has begun!

2 CORINTHIANS 5:17

GOING FURTHER

⊕ In what ways are you a different person now than you were last year? What part has the adventure of faith played in that transformation?

⊕ How easy or difficult is it for you to change?

⊕ What's the first thing that comes to mind when you think of giving up your "old self"?

⊕ What comes to mind when you think of becoming more like Jesus?

⊕ What are you going to do about it?

THE WORD ON OUR TRUE IDENTITY

Take some time to read one or more of the following Bible passages:

Genesis 17:1-6 and 35:9-15; Isaiah 62:2-4; Ezekiel 18:30-32; Matthew 16:13-19; 2 Corinthians 5:14-17; Ephesians 4:21-24

Where
Your Treasure
Is . . .

*When the heart of a dwarf, even the most respectable,
is wakened by gold and by jewels, he grows suddenly bold,
and he may become fierce.*

From Chapter Thirteen of *The Hobbit*

At last Smaug is dead. The dragon may be over-
thrown, but Thorin Oakenshield, King under the
Mountain, now has a far greater enemy to face
than the armies waiting at his door: *greed*. Tolkien

calls it the "dragon-sickness." Whatever its name, it has Thorin by the gut, and he will not bend to the demands of men or elves. Thus the Battle of Five Armies begins—the unexpected fiasco at the culminating point of Bilbo's adventure.

At the center of the struggle is the famed Arkenstone, the great treasure of the dwarves that has been lost and that Thorin is determined to find at any cost. While it's clear the hoard doesn't have quite the hold on Bilbo that it has on the dwarves, it still grips him on some level. When he sees the Arkenstone, he can't resist the temptation to keep it for himself, and later he can hardly bear to give it up. In a way, the Arkenstone is an eerie forerunner to the One Ring in *The Lord of the Rings,* a treasure of great value that claims the hearts of its owners and will not let them go. Incidentally, Bilbo's willingness to give up the Arkenstone at the end of *The Hobbit* is an important foreshadowing of events in subsequent tales, though Tolkien didn't know it at the time.

But let's talk about this notion of "dragon-sickness" for a moment. We've already discussed our need for creature comforts; yet the quest for treasure—for flashy stuff we don't need—is another matter altogether. When we were toddlers, one of the first things we learned how to say (after "No!") was "Mine!"—especially if we had siblings who regularly threatened our territory. That's why one of the most important things we were taught in preschool was how to share. Unfortunately, working against all this good training are the values of popular culture. Our money-hungry, grasping society has given us the impression that the ultimate quest is to become richer and richer as life goes on—"upwardly mobile," as they say. We must have the Arkenstones of this world—the nicer cars, the bigger houses, the luxury vacations—or nothing.

In short, our whole culture, including many Christians, is under the spell of "dragon-sickness." One of the first symptoms is denial that we're under the spell. Another is ongoing discontent with what we have. Still another is the occasional pang of jealousy when someone has what we don't. Sound familiar?

In Catholicism, greed (or avarice) is considered one of the seven deadly sins (behavior that holds the seeds of self-destruction). Thorin is the perfect example of the three main things greed can destroy: (1) our good sense, (2) our relationships, and (3) our self-respect.

First, greed affects the mind, the ability to reason. Tolkien uses words like "bewitchment" and "bewilderment" to express the effect of the hoard on the dwarves. Even Bilbo experiences a touch of the sickness during the Riddle Game with Smaug. The hobbit becomes confused and begins to suspect—at Smaug's suggestion—that the dwarves are planning to cheat him out of his share of the treasure. Later, he manages to justify keeping the Arkenstone for himself. Greed paralyzes our ability to reason things out, to take the other point of view, to weigh the pros and cons in a given situation. It makes us suspicious, paranoid, and alarmist.

Second, greed affects our relationships. That's because we lose sight of what's really important: the love and loyalty of our family and peers. We've seen this principle at work in our own lives, for there's no underestimating the damaging effects of unresolved financial issues between friends. And we see it in the character of Thorin. His unreasonable behavior creates a wedge between him and everyone else—not only the elves and the people of Lake Town, but also the dwarves in his own company. He nearly kills Bilbo upon discovering that the hobbit gave the treasured stone away. It's only on Thorin's deathbed, when his mind is cleared by pain and shame, that he's able to restore his relationship with Bilbo and acknowledge the rightness and honesty of the hobbit's decision.

Finally, greed makes you lose your dignity and self-respect. When you calculate your worth by how much treasure you have in your hoard, you lose sight of your inherent value as a human being, which is where dignity comes from, whether you're rich or poor. When you finally wake up and realize how foolish you've been about your greedy desires, you feel shame: the pain at having lost the respect of those whose opinions matter most to you.

Yes, for all of us, the sickness of greed runs deep as thirst and is not cured by being quenched. The more you have, the more you want; it's one of the spiritual laws of the universe, counter-intuitive as it sounds. You would think it'd be the other way around: the more you have, the less you want. But no, the rules are reversed when it comes to wealth and possessions.

For this reason, Jesus spoke about money and wealth perhaps more than any other subject besides God. Upon hearing his hyperbolic state-ment about how difficult it is for the rich to enter heaven, the disciples asked in astonishment, "Then who in the world can be saved?" (see

Matthew 19:23-26). In other words, they recognized the pull of wealth and the sin of greed in their own lives and were well aware of its power to steer a person off track from pursuing the adventure of faith altogether.

Jesus also warned, "Don't store up treasures here on earth, where they can be eaten by moths and get rusty, and where thieves break in and steal. Store your treasures in heaven, where they will never become moth-eaten or rusty and where they will be safe from thieves. Wherever your treasure is, there your heart and thoughts will also be" (Matthew 6:19-21).

When it comes to this principle as expressed in the pages of *The Hobbit*, it's Bilbo who realizes that Thorin's heart *is* the Arkenstone. While Thorin's desire for the stone has the potential to be his saving grace as a bargaining tool, it proves to be his downfall. Yet before he dies, Thorin has the humility to seek reconciliation with Bilbo. Not only does he ask forgiveness for his foolish behavior, he acknowledges the beauty and simplicity of Bilbo's contented way of life: "If more of us valued food and cheer and song above hoarded gold, it would be a merrier world."[36]

Hobbits care little for great treasures and are happy enough just to be in a snug home by the fire, with a kettle of tea. Bilbo might be an adventurous fellow, and he won't turn down the opportunity to take a little treasure home when the time comes, but he doesn't throw away his sanity, his friendships, or his dignity in the quest. And neither should we.

Beware! Don't be greedy for what you don't have. Real life is not measured by how much we own.

LUKE 12:15

GOING FURTHER

⊕ How do you feel when a friend or family member owes you money but won't admit it? How does this person's behavior create a wedge in your relationship?

⊕ How often do your friends express discontent
because of something they want but don't have?
How often do you?

⊕ When it comes to what this life has to offer,
how content are you with the simple pleasures
God gives?

⊕ What is the true treasure in your life?

⊕ What are you going to do about it?

THE WORD ON REAL TREASURE

Take some time to read one or more of the following
Bible passages:

Proverbs 22:1; Ecclesiastes 5:18-20; Jeremiah 9:23-24;
Matthew 13:44-46 and 19:16-26; Luke 12:13-15;
1 Timothy 6:6-10 and 6:17-19

CHAPTER TWENTY-ONE

ADVENTURE'S END

"This is a bitter adventure, if it must end so;
and not a mountain of gold can amend it."

BILBO TO THORIN, CHAPTER EIGHTEEN OF *The Hobbit*

Throughout *The Lord of the Rings*, both Sam and Frodo often make reference to Mr. Bilbo's adventure during the course of their own dangerous journey through Middle-earth. Bilbo is a simple hobbit, like them—not some powerful leader among the Wise of Middle-earth. And though

Bilbo's story is mixed with tragedy and not all the main characters come to a good end, the overall tone is one of victory over evil, a comedy in the truest classical sense. What better tale for them to cling to as they face the darkness of Mordor?

It's not hard to imagine that Bilbo—in telling his adventures to anyone who would listen—glosses over just how hopeless the Battle of Five Armies felt at the time. In the thick of it, no one is sure of the outcome, and Bilbo wishes he were "well out of it." Then afterward, when summoned to Thorin's side as the dwarf is dying, Bilbo expresses what so many of us feel when gripped by grief or failure: that it's a "bitter adventure" indeed, if this is how things turn out.

Too often, life feels more like a tragedy than a comedy. Even the adventure of faith itself is a strange, painful mix of joy and sorrow, victory and defeat. At times we might lose close friends through miscommunication, separation, or devastating illness. Maybe a new, exciting ministry falls flat after only a few months or vicious gossip destroys the credibility of a campus Bible study. Perhaps a family member quits walking with Jesus altogether. Sometimes there's no clear-cut ending to the various chapters of our story, and we often wonder what God is up to. What sort of tale have we fallen into? Does the Author really know what he's doing? Will he bring our adventure to a good end? It's hard to understand when we're in the middle of it.

In one of Tolkien's letters, he says, "the Writer of the Story is not one of us."[37] The Author at the helm of this whole adventure is not someone who quits what he started, like so many of us (like Tolkien himself, who would have given up on *The Lord of the Rings,* if it hadn't been for the encouragement of his friend C. S. Lewis!). God calls himself "the Alpha and the Omega—the Beginning and the End" (Revelation 21:6)— *alpha* being the first letter in the Greek alphabet and *omega* being the last. In other words, God successfully completes what he sets out to accomplish, including the adventure of our faith.

For proof, we can simply look at Jesus. His death—while it seemed at the time like a bad end to what could have been a marvelous tale— was not the final chapter in God's story. It was, however, the completion of all Jesus had set out to do from the beginning, which is why, as he breathed his last, he was able to say, "It is finished!" (John 19:30). And to his disciples— who all along had failed to understand their Lord's true aims—it certainly felt over. A humiliating execution was the worst possible way to finish a life, and the disciples must have assumed that all their hopes, all their great plans, had indeed come to a bad end.

But the story itself wasn't finished. The adventure of faith continued when Jesus rose from the dead three days later, and it continues today in each one of our lives.

The greatest tale is one that we're a part of still, even as the centuries pass, and it's one that will continue long after we're gone. As we walk this road, which seems dark sometimes, we recognize that others—heroes out of the old stories—have traveled this way before. Peter, John, Mary, Martha, and the others all took the path that is Christ himself. And other adventurers will follow in our footsteps someday.

Meanwhile, we could choose to be like Thorin and balk at the good end—the right path—when it's placed before us. We could go our own way and create more tragedy for ourselves and for others. Yet God does not abandon the overall direction of his story just because one of his characters messes up. Whether we are his willing assistants or not, and even with our best attempts to thwart his plans, he still brings them about. He will use others in our place if we refuse to cooperate, but God's story *will* arrive at its happy ending someday. And it's up to us to choose whether or not we'll be a part of it.

As we've already mentioned, Tolkien wrote to his son Christopher, "Keep up your hobbitry in heart." He then added, "And think that all *stories* feel like that when you are *in* them. You are inside a very great story!"[38]

So if you've been thinking lately that you'll never be able to finish this faith business—or if you've been wondering whether this tale you've "fallen into" is a tragedy after all—don't give in. God finishes what he starts. And he never would have set you on this adventure of faith in the first place unless he intended to bring it to its proper ending. Like Sam and Frodo, who are able to take heart in the midst of dark times by remembering Bilbo's tale, we too can keep in mind that we are "inside a very great story!"—one that has a happy ending.

I am sure that God, who began the good work within you, will continue his work until it is finally finished on that day when Christ Jesus comes back again.

PHILIPPIANS 1:6

GOING FURTHER

⊕ If you could ask God one question in the midst
of tragedy, what would it be?

⊕ What reassurance do you have that God intends
to bring your life to a "good end"? What role
do you play in bringing about that good end?

⊕ What are the tales and stories that give you strength
to keep going?

⊕ How can your life be a story that encourages others?

⊕ What are you going to do about it?

THE WORD ON OUR ADVENTURE'S END

Take some time to read one or more of the following
Bible passages:

*Psalm 139:1-18; Hebrews 10:32-39 and 12:1-3;
James 1:12; Revelation 21:5-7*

HOME AT LAST

*He was now weary of his adventure. He was aching
in his bones for the homeward journey.*

FROM CHAPTER EIGHTEEN OF *The Hobbit*

For most of his adventure, in some form or
another, Bilbo longs for his hobbit-hole (count
how many times he dreams of food and wishes
he were back at Bag-End!). And we can't really
blame him. The journey to the Lonely Mountain
has been far more adventurous than even Gandalf

anticipated, and our hero is a very little fellow—
not to mention he's a Baggins. So we're really not
surprised—once the treasure is found and the
conflict ended—that Bilbo's quest turns away
from all of those things and back toward the
Shire. Going home becomes his main drive. And
though he isn't prepared for what he finds there,
he's able to settle down eventually and regain
something of his former life.

Then in the opening scenes of *The Lord of the
Rings* we learn that Bilbo has become restless
again. It's been over fifty years since his return
from the adventures in *The Hobbit,* and he senses
that he's getting old. While he dearly loves the
Shire—particularly Bag-End—he can't help
longing for the one place where he experienced
true rest: Rivendell, the abode of Master Elrond,
the Last Homely House on the Edge of the
Wild.

Tolkien writes that Elrond's house "was
perfect, whether you liked food, or sleep, or
work, or story-telling, or singing, or just sitting

and thinking best, or a pleasant mixture of them all."[39] Even as Frodo sets out on the dangerous mission into Mordor, Bilbo is settling down in retirement in Rivendell. For him, the Last Homely House will indeed be the last home, the last house he has on Middle-earth before he leaves with the ships at the end.

The Last Homely House. Sounds lovely, doesn't it? Think of yourself when you're utterly exhausted, perhaps after a long day on the job or at the end of a mission trip, when all you want is a shower and a bed and a good meal. What sort of place would you want to come home to? For some of us, it isn't the place we have at the moment, whatever and wherever that may be. Not all of us have a lovely, relaxing landing pad to go to at the end of the day. In fact, some of us might be tempted to go on adventures—including the adventure of faith—for the precise reason that we're desperate to get away from home as soon as possible. Parents are fighting, roommates annoy us, the place is a mess, or we're treated like slave

labor—whatever. For some, home adds stress
and tension to life; it's not a safe or comfy place.

Yet something in all of us longs for the real
deal, a genuine place of comfort and security,
where we can be ourselves. That's because we're
born with the longing for home, a longing that
is never satisfied until we're in God's presence
forever. Psalm 90:1 puts it this way: "Lord,
through all the generations you have been our
home!" In God's presence there is safety, nourishment, strength—and above all, rest. God
himself is our home.

Jesus—despite the fact that he was basically
homeless and called his disciples to a life of
constant travel—assured his followers that home
is what God has in store for those who follow
him. He said, "There are many rooms in my
Father's home, and I am going to prepare a place
for you" (John 14:2). We will work and work
and work in this lifetime until our eyes are weak
and our bones are weary, and all for the Kingdom
of God. But one day we'll be ushered into God's

presence, and he will say, "Well done, my good and faithful servant" (Matthew 25:21). And it's not hard to imagine we'll be given rest and nourishment and whatever work is ours to do, the kind of work that never exhausts our strength but instead energizes us—rather like Bilbo writing the account of his adventure once it's over.

Of course, what we're really talking about is heaven. Not the goofy, cartoon version of "paradise," with clouds and halos and harps. But *home,* where those we love and the Father we adore are gathered in one place—perhaps for a splendid party, complete with storytelling and singing and a good night's rest. And there our Host will be, the Captain of all our mad adventures; and there too will be all those faithful companions who gave up everything to follow him. And we will laugh and remember the various chapters of our wonderful story and marvel at the way God brought comedy out of tragedy.

But until that day, heaven is the Last Homely House that we long for as Christians. Eventually

we realize that we're never really at home anywhere in this life—and we had better not get
too comfortable here, either, as we've discussed
in previous chapters. If we ever feel at home
on earth, it's because we're getting a small taste
of what our true home in heaven will be like.

In the meantime, we have work to do. We
have an adventure to go on, a role to play in this
great story that we've "fallen into" with Jesus.
Our existence will not be safe, comfortable,
or predictable for a good long while—at least
not until all the tales have been written and all
the old songs and stories have come true. Then
someday, when our adventures are over, like
Bilbo we'll be able to say, "Our back is to legends
and we are coming home."[40]

*Surely your goodness and unfailing love will pursue
me all the days of my life, and I will live in the house
of the Lord forever.*

PSALM 23:6

GOING FURTHER

⊕ When are you most exhausted? If you could rest and relax anywhere, where would it be?

⊕ What is your image of heaven?

⊕ How does it feel, knowing that Jesus has gone on "to prepare a place for you" in God's presence?

⊕ What are some ways you can share the hope of heaven with those who long for rest?

⊕ What are you going to do about it?

THE WORD ON GOING HOME

Take some time to read one or more of the following Bible passages:

Matthew 11:28-30; John 14:1-7; 2 Corinthians 5:1-9; Hebrews 4:1-11; Revelation 21:3-4

quick reference guide

A Glossary of Terms Related to
The Hobbit *and* The Lord of the Rings

Arkenstone   The greatest of the lost treasures of the dwarves, which they hope to recover in the expedition to the Lonely Mountain.

Bag-End   Also known as The Hill: a cozy hobbit-hole in a hill; home to Bilbo Baggins and later to his heir, Frodo; located in the Shire.

Battle of Five Armies   The climactic event of *The Hobbit,* in which men, elves, and dwarves are forced to unite against an attack of evil goblins and wargs (wolves).

Beorn   A daunting man who can change into a bear. He becomes a "fierce friend" of Gandalf, Bilbo, and the dwarves.

Bilbo Baggins   The unlikely hero of *The Hobbit,* the "chosen and selected burglar" who travels with a company of dwarves to steal back treasure from the dragon Smaug. See *Hobbits.*

Dark Lord   See *Necromancer.*

Dragons   Huge winged creatures from the North of Middle-earth that hoard treasure and destroy enemies with fire. See *Smaug.*

Dwarves   Short manlike creatures, thirteen of which appear on Bilbo's doorstep at the beginning of *The Hobbit:*

Dwalin, Balin, Kili, Fili, Dori, Nori, Ori, Óin, Gloin, Bifur, Bofur, Bombur, and their leader, Thorin Oakenshield. They are determined to reclaim their treasure from Smaug and restore Thorin as the rightful king.

Edge of the Wild   The dividing line between the known lands of Middle-earth to the West and the unknown lands to the East.

Elrond   Also known as Master Elrond, the wise, half-elven leader who lives in the Last Homely House in Rivendell on the Edge of the Wild. He helps Bilbo, Gandalf, and the dwarves in *The Hobbit* and plays a large role in *The Lord of the Rings.*

Elvenking   The king of the Wood-elves whose palace is on the edge of Mirkwood Forest. He imprisons the dwarves when they refuse to tell him their mission. In *The Fellowship of the Ring,* we learn he is the father of Legolas the Elf.

Elves   The firstborn among the created beings of Middle-earth. They have a long-standing feud with the dwarves.

Elvish   Several dialects of an imaginary language invented by J. R. R. Tolkien. The languages were conceived before the characters, history, and topography of Middle-earth.

Frodo   The chosen heir of Bilbo Baggins and hero of *The Lord of the Rings.*

Gandalf   The wise wizard in charge of the expedition to the Lonely Mountain. He then plays a starring role in *The Lord of the Rings,* eventually revealing himself to be an emissary (something of an "angel") sent to aid the good forces of Middle-earth.

Gloin   One of the thirteen dwarves in the expedition to the Lonely Mountain. In *The Fellowship of the Ring*, we learn he is the father of Gimli the Dwarf.

Goblins   Also known as "orcs." Evil creatures that live under the Misty Mountains and attack Bilbo and the dwarves.

Gollum   An ancient creature who lives in the dark under the Misty Mountains. He is in possession of the Ring but loses it, and Bilbo accidentally finds it. Once Bilbo wins the Riddle Game and escapes, Gollum's long obsession to reclaim the Ring begins.

Hobbits   Small people from an obscure corner of Middle-earth, chiefly distinguished by their large, hairy feet; curly hair; and love of good food.

King under the Mountain   Thorin Oakenshield, the dwarf-heir to the kingdom of the Lonely Mountain that has been overtaken by Smaug the dragon. Old songs and tales prophesy that the king will return one day.

Lake Town   The town of men situated on Long Lake not far from the base of the Lonely Mountain.

Last Homely House   The house of Master Elrond in Rivendell on the Edge of the Wild.

Lonely Mountain   A mountain situated in the middle of a large plain near Long Lake. It has been taken over by the dragon Smaug, but is reclaimed by the dwarves at the end of *The Hobbit*.

Long Lake   A lake near the base of the Lonely Mountain on which there is a city of men. Bilbo and the dwarves travel downriver in barrels from the Elvenking's palace to Long Lake.

LOTR junkies   *Lord of the Rings* fanatics who walk around barefoot, debate the merits of *Quenya* versus *Sindarin* Elvish, and watch the extended DVD versions of all three films in a row on a weekly basis.

"Mad Baggins"   The nickname given to Bilbo by his neighbors in reference to his odd adventurous streak.

Master of Lake Town   The foolish leader of the people of the Lake. He is skeptical of Thorin's claim to be the returning king.

Middle-earth   The imaginary land in which *The Hobbit* and *The Lord of the Rings* take place.

Mirkwood   The treacherous forest that lies between the Misty Mountains and Long Lake, full of spiders and other evil creatures. It is also home of the Elvenking.

Misty Mountains   The great chain of mountains running north to south just over the Edge of the Wild. Here Bilbo and later Frodo have dangerous encounters with goblins while attempting to cross over the mountains.

Mordor   The kingdom of the Dark Lord Sauron in *The Lord of the Rings.*

Necromancer   Another word for an evil wizard or magician who has dealings with the dead. This is Tolkien's original term for the Dark Lord Sauron, who is given no name in *The Hobbit*, but whose evil presence is beginning to pose problems for Gandalf and the other good guardians of Middle-earth. Readers of *The Hobbit* were so intrigued by allusions to the Necromancer that they asked Tolkien to write more about him in the next book(!). And Sauron appears as the Great Eye in *The Lord of the Rings*.

Orcs   See *Goblins*.

Riddle Game   The contest between Bilbo and Gollum under the Misty Mountains, in which each poses riddles for the other to solve. If Bilbo fails to solve a riddle, Gollum will eat him. If Gollum fails to solve one, he must show Bilbo the way out. Gollum loses but proves treacherous, and Bilbo barely escapes with his life.

Ring   The object Bilbo finds by accident in the dark of the goblin tunnels. It renders its wearer invisible but seems to be of no greater significance until the events of *The Lord of the Rings* unfold.

Rivendell   The valley where Master Elrond dwells in the Last Homely House, just over the Edge of the Wild.

Sam Gamgee   Frodo Baggins's gardener and companion in *The Lord of the Rings*. Sam never doubts Bilbo's or Frodo's sanity and in fact has an adventurous streak himself.

Sauron   See *Necromancer*.

Shire, The   Land inhabited by hobbits in an obscure, overlooked corner of Middle-earth.

Smaug   The dangerous dragon who has taken over the Lonely Mountain that once belonged to the dwarves. There he hoards stolen treasure and devastates the surrounding land.

Spiders   Nasty inhabitants of Mirkwood Forest that attack the dwarves when they wander off the path.

Thorin Oakenshield The leader of the dwarves, heir to the kingdom under the Lonely Mountain.

Tolkien, J. R. R. Celebrated author of *The Hobbit*, *The Lord of the Rings*, and various other works related to the history and mythology of his imaginary world of Middle-earth.

Took The last name of Bilbo's mother, Belladonna, whose family was known for having an adventurous streak.

Trolls Mean, stupid giants that capture Bilbo and the dwarves shortly after the adventure begins. They turn to stone when the sun rises.

Wargs Evil wolves that trap Bilbo, Gandalf, and the dwarves up in trees after they've escaped from the goblin tunnels.

Wizards Powerful beings that are sent as guardians and leaders for the good forces of Middle-earth. In *The Hobbit*, Gandalf appears as a simple magician to Bilbo's eyes.

Wolves See *Wargs*.

Wood-elves A race of elves that live on the edge of Mirkwood Forest. See *Elvenking*.

NOTES

Introduction

[1] C. S. Lewis, from the introduction to *Lilith* by George MacDonald (Grand Rapids, Mich.: Wm. B. Eerdmans Publishing Co., 1981), x–xi.

[2] See *The Letters of J. R. R. Tolkien,* edited by Humphrey Carpenter (New York: Houghton Mifflin Company, 2000), 288.

[3] Ibid., 172.

[4] Ibid., 262, 297–298.

[5] "The Quest of Erebor" can be found in Appendix A of *The Annotated Hobbit* by J. R. R. Tolkien, annotated by Douglas A. Anderson (New York: Houghton Mifflin Company, 2002).

Chapter 1

[6] J. R. R. Tolkien, *The Hobbit* (New York: Ballantine Books, 1965), 19.

Chapter 2

[7] Connie Rupp and Peter Rupp, *Shackleton and the Endurance* (New York: Scholastic, Inc., 2001), 5.

[8] Tolkien, *Hobbit,* 22.

[9] Tolkien, *Letters,* 215.

Chapter 3

[10] C. S. Lewis was a colleague and friend of J. R. R. Tolkien and author of The Chronicles of Narnia series, including *The Lion, the Witch and the Wardrobe.* He encouraged Tolkien to finish *The Lord of the Rings.*

Chapter 5
[11] Tolkien, *Hobbit,* 293.

Chapter 7
[12] Tolkien, *The Two Towers* (New York: Ballantine Books, 1965), 432.
[13] Tolkien, *Letters,* 78.
[14] Tolkien, *Hobbit,* 212–213.

Chapter 8
[15] For the original version of the story, see margin notations in *The Annotated Hobbit,* 128–131.
[16] See chapter 10, "Portents of Great Significance," in this book.

Chapter 9
[17] J. R. R. Tolkien, *The Fellowship of the Ring* (New York: Ballantine Books, 1965), 93.

Chapter 10
[18] Ibid., 327.

Chapter 11
[19] Madeleine L'Engle, *And It Was Good: Reflections on Beginnings* (Wheaton, Ill.: Harold Shaw Publishers, 1983), 70. L'Engle wrote the award-winning children's book *A Wrinkle in Time.*

Chapter 12
[20] Tolkien, *Hobbit,* 284.
[21] Tolkien, *Letters,* 100.
[22] J. R. R. Tolkien, *The Tolkien Reader* (New York: Ballantine Books, 1966), 88.

Chapter 13
[23] Tolkien, *Hobbit,* 113.
[24] Ibid., 136.

Chapter 15
25 Ibid., 17.
26 Ibid., 91.

Chapter 16
27 Tolkien, *Fellowship,* 368.
28 Tolkien, *Hobbit,* 303.

Chapter 17
29 Ibid., 11.

Chapter 18
30 Ibid., 191.
31 Tolkien, *Towers,* 45.
32 A fellow by the name of Hugo Dyson, who occasionally attended a literary group with Tolkien and Lewis called The Inklings.
33 Tolkien, *Reader,* 89.

Chapter 19
34 Tolkien, *Hobbit,* 271.
35 Ibid., 300.

Chapter 20
36 Ibid., 288.

Chapter 21
37 Tolkien, *Letters,* 252.
38 Ibid., 78.

Chapter 22
39 Tolkien, *Hobbit,* 51.
40 Ibid., 298.

COMING SUMMER 2005 . . .

Dating
Mr. Darcy

The smart girl's guide to
sensible romance

The new book
by Sarah Arthur

fiction.

Sierra's Story 0-8423-8726-9
Ryun's Story 1-4143-0003-4
Kenzie's Story 1-4143-0002-6

Kyra's Story 0-8423-8284-4
Miranda's Story 0-8423-8283-6
Tyrone's Story 0-8423-8285-2

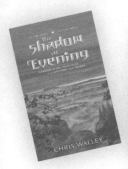

THE LAMB AMONG THE STARS SERIES

The Shadow at Evening 1-4143-0067-0
The Power of the Night 1-4143-0068-9

Other thirsty(?) fiction

Love Rules 0-8423-8727-7
Dear Baby Girl 1-4143-0093-X

nonfiction.

Walk 0-8423-6069-7

Come Clean 0-8423-8358-1

Walking with Frodo 0-8423-8554-1

Walking with Bilbo 1-4143-0131-6

tap into life.

areuthirsty.com

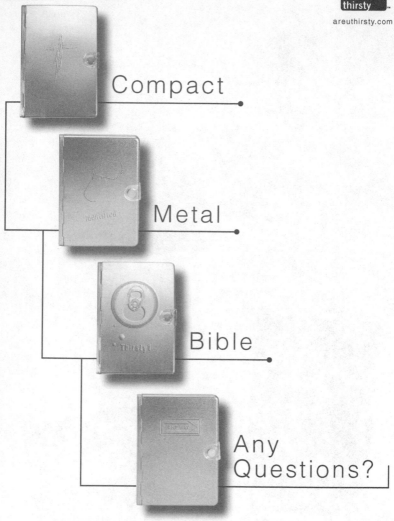

Compact

Metal

Bible

Any
Questions?

Available wherever Bibles are sold

areUthirsty.com

well . . . are you?